THE PARADOXES OF JESUS

✠✠✠✠✠✠✠✠✠✠✠✠✠✠✠✠✠✠✠✠✠✠✠✠✠✠✠✠✠✠✠✠✠✠✠

The Paradoxes of Jesus

RALPH W. SOCKMAN

ABINGDON PRESS
NEW YORK • NASHVILLE

✠✠✠✠✠✠✠✠✠✠✠✠✠✠✠✠✠✠✠✠✠✠✠✠✠✠✠✠✠✠✠✠✠✠✠

THE PARADOXES OF JESUS

Copyright MCMXXXVI by Ralph W. Sockman

PRINTED AND BOUND AT NASHVILLE,
TENNESSEE, UNITED STATES OF AMERICA

To

THE CONGREGATION

OF

CHRIST CHURCH

WHICH WELCOMED THE WRITER

TWENTY-FIVE YEARS AGO AS MEMBER

AND

TWENTY YEARS AGO AS MINISTER

CONTENTS

CONTENTS

FOREWORD

I T is not quite correct to announce that this book grew out of the lectures given at Yale University on the Kent Shaffer Memorial Foundation. More accurate is it to say that those addresses were the outgrowth of queries which had long been germinating in the author's mind.

Seed which falls on the stony ground of the crowded street does not bear as much fruit as that sown in the soil of the cloistered study. But perhaps the product has a peculiar value from the fact that it has survived the surge of city life. These pages do not aim to give a compilation of commentaries or to delve into technical scholarship. They offer a sidewalk survey of that Unforgettable One who himself spoke by the wayside.

It would be impossible to acknowledge by name the aid of all who have contributed to these interpretations. The author feels deeply his debt of gratitude to Mr. John C. Shaffer, the founder of the lectureship, and to the Dean, the Faculty, and the students of the Yale Divinity School for making possible and pleasurable the delivery of the messages; to Professor Burton Scott Easton, and to Miss Sarah F. Hoyt for illuminating insights; to Miss Harriet Seibert, Miss Dorothy Ingling, Mrs. Elmer E. Count, Mrs. Helen Hiller Palmer, Mr. Francis Purcell, and Mr. Eric Lakes, for valuable assistance in the preparation of the manuscripts.

R. W. S.

New York City

TO JESUS THE NAZARENE

Closest to men, thou pitying Son of man,
  And thrilled from crown to foot with fellowship,
  Yet most apart and strange and lonely as God—
  Dwell in my heart, remote and intimate One!
Brother of all the world I come to thee!

Gentle as she who nursed thee at her breast
  (Yet what a lash of lightnings once thy tongue
  To scourge the hypocrite and Pharisee!)
  Nerve thou mine arm, O meek, O mighty One!
Champion of all who fail, I fly to thee!

O man of Sorrows with the wounded hands—
  For chaplet, for throne, a pagan cross;
  Bowed with the woe and agony of time;
  Yet loved by children and the feasting guests—
I bring my suffering, joyful heart to thee!

Chaste as the virginal lily on her stem,
  Yet in each hot, full pulse, each tropic vein,
  More filled with feeling than the flower with sun,
  No anchorite—hale, sinewy, warm with love—
I come in youth's high tide of bliss to thee!

O Christ of contrasts; infinite paradox,
  Yet life's explainer, solvent harmony,
  Frail strength, pure passion, meek austerity,
  And the white splendor of these darkened years—
I lean my wondering, wayward heart on thine!

                    —*Frederick Lawrence Knowles.*

CHAPTER 1

THE SIMPLE GOSPEL

"THE simple gospel" is an expression of peculiar appeal. It strikes our ears with the welcome sound of an old familiar hymn wafted down from the carillon of a cathedral tower amid the noise of a city's traffic. It calls up the picture of a Palestinian Figure whom the common people flocked gladly to hear. It suggests the pure stream of his thought before it became muddied by the theologians and ecclesiastics. It awakens a wistful mood in those for whom the story of Jesus never grows old.

Moreover, "the simple gospel" is what the man on the street says that he would go to hear if the pulpit would only preach it. It is what the layman in the pew asserts that he would prefer to the political and social discourses now passing for sermons. It is the restorative which would revive Christianity, according to those magazine medicine men who write so many obituaries of dead churches. In short, "the simple gospel" is pictured as the oasis of Christ to those who see only a desert in organized Christianity.

But how simple is the gospel of Jesus? To be sure it contains truths so plain and clear that

13

the untrained minds of innocent children can catch and follow them.   There is an air of simplicity about the biographies of Jesus which blows in our fetid sophistications like the fresh breezes from the Galilean hills.   There is an elemental unity about the Gospels which produces a harmony in the portraits taken as wholes.   But when any one of the Synoptic Gospels is treated as a moving picture and not as a portrait, it reveals a succession of scenes often strangely self-contradictory and puzzlingly paradoxical.   A thoughtful person, reading the story of Jesus for the first time, might think of it as a book of riddles.

Jesus, a Son of the synagogue, asserts such reverence for the law and the prophets that he will not destroy "one jot or one tittle" of the established teaching, yet he repeatedly replaces what had been "said by them of old time" with commands of his own so radically different that the defenders of tradition rightly looked upon him as revolutionary.   He comes forth among his fellow men as a Physician, dispensing health and relieving pain, but he almost immediately begins calling for sacrifices which mean self-denial, even death.   Being moved with compassion, he paradoxically offers to comfort men with a cross and to rest them with a yoke.   Not only is he "that strange Man upon his cross"; he is also the strange Man of the easy yoke.

The Galilean who calls for practical service
and silences emotional admirers, nevertheless
rebukes the active Martha, commends the passive
mystical Mary, and praises the woman who
anoints him with what might have been "sold
for three hundred pence, and given to the poor."
In one place Jesus bids men not to be anxious for
the morrow, and in another forbids men to follow
him until they sit down and count the cost. The
teacher who says, "Resist not him that is evil,"
asserts his power and drives out the corrupt
money-changers from the temple of worship.
Although he commands, "Give to him that asketh
thee," Jesus does not comply with the financial
request of the disinherited man, and he slips away
more than once from crowds coming to be healed.
Leaving before men the ideal of self-forgetting
love and saying, "Whosoever would save his life
shall lose it," nevertheless he speaks often about
rewards and makes explicit promises of them.
Rising so far above financial considerations that
his own dependence on money never enters our
thinking, Jesus surprises us with his counsel,
"Make to yourselves friends by means of the mammon of unrighteousness."

Despite the fact that Jesus says to his followers,
"Judge not, that ye be not judged," he himself
pronounces the most stern judgments on the
Pharisees. So severe in his own holiness, he is

tenderly tolerant toward sinners. Proclaiming
a purity which spurns even the lustful look, he
befriends Magdalenes and moral lepers. And
perhaps the outstanding uniquely paradoxical
feature in the character of Jesus is that his saint-
liness is unaccompanied by any sense of his own
sin. It is a characteristic of good men that the
better they are, the more conscious are they of
their shortcomings. Jesus lays emphasis on that
truth in his praise of the "poor in spirit." He repeatedly warns men against the feeling of moral
self-assurance, such as characterized the Pharisees,
for example. Yet in himself he never reveals
that haunting consciousness of sin which inheres
in genuine sainthood.

Certainly, the career of a personality with so
many puzzling aspects can hardly be called a
"simple gospel." And the paradoxical figure of
Jesus is heightened by many of his recorded single
statements which seem self-contradictory. "He
that findeth his life shall lose it; and he that loseth
his life for my sake shall find it," is an enigma
which readers usually try to explain by explaining away. "Blessed are the meek: for they shall
inherit the earth," is an utterance so seemingly
contrary to practical experience that a magazine
some years ago in a spirit of irony offered a
framed copy of this beatitude to any meek man
who made good. "Unto everyone that hath shall

be given; but from him that hath not, even that which he hath shall be taken away from him" is a statement which might be understandable in Wall Street where the wolves grow more shaggy and the lambs are shorn more closely, but such an assertion of progressive inequality sounds out of place on the lips of Jesus, the apostle of justice. Victims of chance, convinced that life is a lottery, might say, "The last shall be first and the first last," but did not Jesus proclaim the unfailing providence of an infinitely just Heavenly Father who keeps track of even the falling sparrows?

Wisdom in ignorance, gain in loss, freedom in bondage, victory in defeat, life in death—such assertions do seem to justify a Papini in calling Jesus "the supreme maker of paradoxes."

Taken in its full sweep, the gospel record of Jesus is the greatest mystery story ever written. In our day when we turn out mystery stories by the ton, writers have become very adept at confusing situations, concealing motives, and creating suspense. After following a number of these modern plots, the reader begins to find the clues whereby he can foretell the outcome. He can be pretty sure that the characters who look the most innocent will prove the most vicious, and the ones who invite the most suspicion will turn out to be the most virtuous. In short, the way to solve so many mystery plots is merely to reverse the obvious. But the puzzling situations of the gospel are not solved so simply. Jesus did not always speak in riddles which had to be reversed. Often his words were so patently practical that his hearers nodded their heads in admiring assent. His very reasonableness heightens the color of those occasions when he seemed so impractical that his own friends said, "He is beside himself." The story of Jesus is not that of a poor carpenter who triumphs over difficulties and becomes rich, but of a Carpenter who dies "poor, yet making many rich." The Gospels give not the picture of an oppressed peasant who turned the tables on his persecutors and defeated them, but they show us One who claimed to be overcoming the world while it was succeeding in crucifying him.

But what makes the gospel surpass the mysteries of fiction and the paradoxical careers of other historical figures is not the way it ends but the fact that it has not ended. The up-country Leader who was killed during a Jewish Passover was more alive as a factor on the streets of Jerusalem forty days after his death than in the days of his flesh. And the story of Jesus is still running in serial form, to be read in new chapters of healed bodies and changed lives. The supreme paradox of the Palestinian is that he was killed but refuses to die.

CHAPTER II

THE EVADERS OF THE UNAVOIDABLE

IN approaching these puzzles of portraiture, we must take cognizance of various efforts made to resolve the paradoxes of Jesus. One avenue of escape from difficult passages is to say that Jesus may have been incorrectly quoted. It is not within the province of these chapters to explore the field of textual criticism. We shall content ourselves with accepting current accredited scholarship as to the authenticity of the utterances quoted.

In doing so we recognize that "the Gospels were devotional documents rather than documented biographies. They were neither written nor read originally as sources of information, but as sources of religious light and strength. In the Gospels the story of Jesus is drafted very simply but very surely into the service of practical Christian piety."[1] The coloration of the record by the personality and purpose of the author is an old theme which cannot be discussed here.

It seems only reasonable to think, however, that the paradoxical passages of the Gospels would be

---

[1] W. E. Bundy, *Our Discovery of Jesus*, p. 95. Dodd, Mead and Company.

the parts least open to the suspicion of invention. As Chesterton ironically points out, invention is for use, and the fact that men have not yet learned to use so many of Jesus' puzzling counsels precludes the charge that they were invented by his followers. Furthermore, the devotional purpose of the documents would predispose the writers against those seeming contradictions in the record. The natural tendency would have been to trim down to fit the simple consistencies. Hence the normal inference of the reader is that these difficult paradoxes have a special claim to credence.

A second easy way around the "hard sayings" of Jesus is to focus the eye on only one phase of the paradox involved. Sometimes this is done through ignorance and sometimes through inclination. Many readers of the New Testament do not read far enough or conscientiously enough to comprehend the links in the record or to feel the difficulties in linking the passages together. The majority of modern church members treat the Scripture somewhat as sentimental maidens treat wedding cake—that is, they break it into small pieces and sleep on it. Their knowledge of Jesus is just a collection of unrelated pictures. Not taking the pains to put them together, they do not experience the strain of harmonizing them.

Others there are who see only those facets of Jesus' many-sided character which appeal to their particular interest or need. Some welcome Jesus' teaching on health and happiness, but, like the Palestinian crowds, they turn away from his words about sacrifice and the cross. Seeing only the healing Physician, they have no difficulty in reconciling him with the suffering Servant. Some hear only the Jesus who talks about peace of mind and have their ears closed to him when he bids men turn the other cheek in order to have peace among men. Such one-sided listeners are not conscious of the paradox of a "peace of God which passeth all understanding." Others read the Master's words of practical wisdom and feel that they have discovered a hitherto hidden executive Genius who would make a success in Wall Street. But in playing up Jesus as a man of affairs whom nobody knows, they overlook Jesus, the Man of Sorrows, who for some reason remained poorer than the foxes of the field for he had "not where to lay his head."

This attitude of taking what we want of Jesus' teaching and ignoring the rest gains for us neither its full meaning nor its full service. We cannot commute into the circle of Jesus' audience as suburbanites commute into a city for purposes of business or recreation, while they keep their residence outside. Those whom Jesus counted

his disciples are those who "abide" in his words.
If we cannot see his colossal figure "steadily and
see it whole," we must strive our best to do so.
We must try to see the Jesus of the wedding supper as well as the Jesus of the Last Supper, the
comrade with his arms locked in joyous fellowship
with others as well as the blood-drained Figure
with a spear thrust in his side, the great High
Priest lifting the faltering prayers of his frightened followers to God as well as the Captain of
our salvation crying on the field of life's battle
that he "came not to send peace, but a sword."

When we stand before the baffling contrasts in
the conduct and words of Jesus, we cannot cut
our way through by cutting the paradoxes in two
and taking the parts which suit our theories.

Another way around the "hard sayings" of Jesus
is that taken by those modern writers who say
that the aim of Jesus was to give only an "interim-
ethik." We are told that, like those around him,
Jesus expected the world as it now is to come to
an end soon and to be replaced by a new order,
a kingdom of God in which conditions would be
changed. Hence his aim was to teach men how
to order their lives during the little time that was
left to them. This would explain some of his
extreme counsels and excuse us from finding
in them a continuing validity.

It must be admitted that the idea of a cataclysmic end of the world characterized Jewish thought of Jesus' day. This belief persisted and deepened in the days of Jerusalem's destruction, the period in which the Synoptic Gospels were taking shape. How far the established passages attributed to Jesus, in our translation were actually his own utterances, and how far they were read into his remembered sayings by the writers are open questions which will probably never be closed.

Certainly, Jesus did use the current apocalyptic beliefs as the framework for some of his teaching. It is hard to see how he could have gripped the minds of his hearers otherwise. They knew nothing about our modern theories of evolutionary process. They read in their Scriptures that the world had been created suddenly by divine fiat, and how else could a new age come into being? The preacher of a new kingdom would have been unintelligible to them if he had talked in our terms of building a new order by long social programs. Moreover, are not our own maturer ideas of evolutionary change coming to take more cognizance of crises? We are seeing ever more clearly that growth and progress have their recessions and their rapids, their periods when "the kingdom of heaven suffereth violence" (Matthew 11. 12).

There was an undeniable urgency about Jesus' expectation of change. Surveying the contemporary scene, he saw the forces converging toward a crisis in his own country. For Judaism it was the end of an era. And what is more, Jesus' vivid sense of a living God gave to him an expectancy of divine intervention. History to him is no mere succession of human efforts and events but, rather, an interplay between men and God.

Hence Jesus did incorporate the apocalyptic element in his teaching as a vehicle not only to reach his hearers but also to convey the sense of vitalizing urgency which he himself felt. Nevertheless, his general message was in inward contradiction to a cataclysmic coming of the Kingdom. He warned the Pharisees against fretting themselves over the date of its coming "for lo, the kingdom of God is within you" (Luke 17. 21). Again and again he tried to make men realize that the new order of life was a present reality. "But if I by the Spirit of God cast out devils, then is the kingdom of God come upon you" (Matthew 12. 28). When he said that "he that is but little in the kingdom of heaven is greater than" John the Baptist, Jesus was certainly referring to the Kingdom in the sense of a present accompaniment and not in the sense of a final fate. Furthermore, Jesus had a fundamental optimism about God's present control which was in basic contrast to the pessimism which provoked the current expectation of world overthrow.

No, the apocalyptic elements in the Gospels do not serve to confine Jesus' moral precepts to a brief period back in the first century. Professor Ernest F. Scott concedes that the "interim conception colored some of Jesus' sayings on renunciation." They were spoken for the direction of his followers in the unique emergency which was now, he believed, in front of them. To insist on their permanent validity would be much the same as to place on the statute-book orders that were issued in time of war.[2] And the late Dean Bosworth admits that the apocalyptic "view of the situation may have occasionally affected the application of his fundamental ethical principles to concrete situations, particularly in the case of the use of property."[3] But, further than this, both assert that the theory of "interim-ethik" may be confidently put aside.

How far we can admit that even the teachings on property and renunciation were meant for an "interim" will appear later. But as for Jesus' difficult paradoxes in general, we cannot dispose of them by saying that they were meant only for an emergency period in the distant past.

[2] Ernest F. Scott, *The Ethical Teaching of Jesus*, p. 53. The Macmillan Company, New York.
[3] Edward I Bosworth, *The Life and Teachings of Jesus*, p. 254. The Macmillan Company, New York.

A fourth way of resolving the hard paradoxes of Jesus is to remove them from the realm of realistic application. This tendency makes itself felt in more than one direction. We may, for one thing, say, as certain German nationalists have been claiming, that "there can be spheres of life in which we do not belong to him, but to other masters."[4] That is a heresy held not only by those nationalists who exempt nations from the application of Christ's ethics, but also by those practical business men who regard the market place as a province outside the reach of a first-century Jewish Carpenter. In fact, almost all of us have certain areas which are No Man's Land for Jesus. Very few of us are Christianized in all our compartments of life and thought. And it is very convenient to dispose of a troublesome command of Jesus by assigning it to one of the exempt zones.

It must be admitted that Jesus seemed to regard some of his more drastic demands as designed for the few rather than for all and as derived from the peculiar situation in which he found himself. Such, for example, was his reference to celibacy. "All men cannot receive this saying, but they to whom it is given" (Matthew 19. 11). As Pro-

---

[4] Proclamation of the Confessional Synod, June, 1934, as reported in *The Church-State Struggle in Germany*, by Henry Smith Leiper, p. 6. Published by American Section: Universal Christian Council for Life and Work.

fessor Burton Scott Easton has pointed out, Jesus in his ethical demands distinguished between the "Kingdom level" to which he sought to raise those fitted for special discipleship, and the "Father level" to which lower plane the general following could be adapted. There was an ethics of vocation expected of the comparatively few.

It is one thing, however, for Jesus to say that some of his commands were meant only for certain persons; it is quite another for an individual to divide his own life into departments and to determine for himself which are to be subject to the sovereignty of Jesus. The latter is a form of that divided loyalty which Jesus declared to be impossible. "No man can serve two masters." Moral chaos results when a man regards his citizenship, his politics, his business, or any other sphere of activity as outside the pale of a central unifying control.

The different paradoxes of Jesus cannot be put out of the way as an interior decorator removes a piece of period furniture to secure harmony.

And what shall be said of those who would remove certain of Jesus' injunctions from troublesome realism by regarding them as Oriental hyperbole possessing a certain pedagogical value but irrelevant to our world of actuality? Is Jesus' teaching of love for one's enemies a counsel of perfection, beautiful to look at like a star in the

heavens but not a moral mountain peak for climbing? Or, in the words of a well-known writer,
"This notion of the supreme worth of the individual is as far beyond any realization today as Einstein's mathematics is beyond the use of the
paper-hanger measuring off the wall paper in my
living room." [5] In view of which separating dis-
tance, the author concludes that religion must
either come forward with a blueprint of a social
order wherein the individual is given supreme
worth—a realization which he holds impossible—
or recognize the irrelevancy of this ideal to modern
society.

When Jesus gave the Beatitudes, was he giving
the blueprints of character for the citizenry of that
new age to come, and did he know that such
characters could not possibly be at home in this
present world? Was the Sermon on the Mount
only the deception of a beautiful mirage to lure
the pilgrim across the desert that now is?

When Jesus said, "Resist not him that is evil,"
he laid down a lovely ideal of brotherly action,
but certainly it seems impracticable in the world
as now constituted. In this age of gangsters and
bullies and dictators, it is the strong arm which
holds in check the rough and ruinous elements;
it is an enlarged navy which Britain believes will

---

[5] Paul Hutchinson, *The Ordeal of Western Religion*, p. 59.
Houghton Mifflin Co.

bring swashbuckling dictators of Europe to their senses. To take Christ literally and to resist not the evil one would be to leave the world at the mercy of the rabble and the ruffians. So men think.

When Jesus said, "Give to him that asketh thee, and from him that would borrow of thee turn not thou away," we are told that he certainly could not have been laying down a rule to be taken literally. Jesus had to walk roads lined with beggars just as we have our appeals for help at every corner. Indiscriminate giving would quickly exhaust the resources of the giver and demoralize the characters of the recipients. Did not Jesus realize this? To say No would be to cast reflection on his intelligence. Did Jesus bid men give because he himself was without funds? To say Yes would be to reflect on his sincerity.

Jesus counseled men, "Be not therefore anxious, saying, What shall we eat? or, What shall we drink? or, Wherewithal shall we be clothed?" And then to inspire such freedom from anxiety he cited God's care of the birds and the flowers. If we were to take the injunction literally and give no worry to our tomorrows, we too might have enough to live on as do the birds of the air, but it would be a mere animal existence far below the much-cited American standard of living with "two cars in every garage and a bird in every pot."

No, some say, the commands of Jesus are coun-

sels of perfection—"Be ye therefore perfect, even
as your Father which is in heaven is perfect"—
but we are living in an imperfect age and we have
to keep our feet on the ground. We are not
dwellers on the stars of a future divine era but
straphangers on the subways where we confront
not theories but two-hundred-pound facts and
where nonresistance means not riding.

That, in substance, is what many of our contemporaries say about the practicability of Jesus'
ethics. And, paradoxically enough, many who
say it are those who claim to "believe the Bible
from cover to cover." Many a layman who would
vote to dismiss his minister if the latter should
question the virgin birth, would call the same
minister a foolish dreamer if he claimed Jesus'
ethical injunctions were to be taken literally.
These orthodox heretics are numerous in our day.

And what is the answer to this charge that
Jesus' morality is not relevant to our world? We
admit that Jesus laid down his counsels as principles, not as rules. A rule resembles the command
of a superior officer to be carried out literally
with an eye on the law rather than on the situation. A principle is a policy of action to be interpreted and applied in line with a general purpose
and in relation to particular situations. The
distinction is observable in the work of a physician. He has certain rules in his practice, to be

sure. But when he comes into a sick-room, it is principles rather than rules which guide him most. The individuality of the patient, the peculiar phases of the particular case may cause him to alter his rules in pursuing his principles of healing. Similarly, Jesus the Physician emphasized principles as above rules.

Thus when he said, "Give to him that asketh thee," Jesus meant that we were to apply the principle of generous love to each request. He laid down a fixed principle but no fixed rules of giving. His own responses to requests show how the methods of applying his principle varied. When the man came to him saying, "Bid my brother divide the inheritance with me," Jesus did not give him what he asked. He said, "Beware of covetousness." To give a person what he requests is not always the best application of generosity. Jesus' principle of reverence for personality requires doing what is best for the supplicant.

A Canaanitish woman came once asking him to come and heal her daughter. At first Jesus answered her not a word. Then in reply to her repeated requests, he is recorded as having spoken one of his darkest sayings: "I was not sent but unto the lost sheep of the house of Israel. . . . It is not meet to take the children's bread and cast it to the dogs" (Matthew 15. 24, 26). Such words sound harshly and narrowly paradoxical on the

lips of Him who told the parable of the good
Samaritan. In the end he did grant her request,
but that answer of his revealed the principle of
specialization in giving, necessary to effectiveness
in the work of Jesus as of others. Matthew's account suggests the strategy of limiting the Master's
work at first to his own people before expanding
it to the Gentiles. It is better to concentrate and
do some things well than to scatter indiscrimi-
nately and therefore ineffectually.

Or, again, we observe Jesus in those early days
of his popularity as a healer when great crowds
followed him. They brought their sick, even
letting them down through the roof. Did Jesus
respond to the pleas of all who besought him?
No. More than once we read of Jesus slipping
away from the throngs to places of solitude and
prayer. Sometimes we can give our best to people
only by running away from their immediate requests and recouping our resources so that we
may have more to give.

In all these situations the principle of giving
was fixed and steady as the ray of sunlight. But
the rules of applying it varied as the colors
brought out by the sun's rays when they fall on
the green grass, the purple cloud, the red rose.

If Jesus had tried to expand his principles into
rules by defining specific methods for special situations, he would have repeated the mistake of

Hebrew legalism. The more intricate their net-work of legislation, the more loopholes for question and casuistry. Furthermore, he would have reduced his daring paradoxes which stab minds awake into dull, platitudinous codes which put consciences to sleep. How the ever-fresh beauty of the Beatitudes would have been pressed out of them by codifying them into a book of detailed rules! Or suppose that in place of the sharp surgical saying, "If thine eye offend thee, pluck it out," Jesus had substituted a long list of the objects which it was best not to look at. Had Jesus hedged his principles about with qualifications and provisos, he would have killed their spirit and crippled their power to cling to our memories. He was not a lawgiver; he was a life-giver. Therefore he laid down principles, not rules.

Does this admission bring us back, then, to the position of those who say that Jesus' counsels are merely beautiful ideals useful for inspiration but not meant for practice? No. Jesus gave us standards, not merely ideals. Which is the more exacting to a conscientious man, a principle or a rule? Which makes the higher demands on us, love or law?

Consider the employee whose hours and rules are prescribed. Later he becomes the head of the business, responsible to his stockholders, his employees, and the public. No time schedule and no code of rules are laid down for him. He is simply expected to follow one central principle, that of doing the best he can to make the most of the business. But if he is a conscientious man, his sense of responsibility will prove far more exacting than any set of rules held over him. It is safe to say that many a time he will look back longingly to the period when he had someone to tell him what to do and how to do it. In the darkest days of the depression, even our biggest bankers seemed glad when the government took over control and relieved them of the strain involved in carrying out their obligations. Yes, the living up to principles requires more thought and more effort than does the following of rules. The application of principles has no upper limit and when the sky is the limit a conscientious person always feels that he should be climbing.

Or turn to the realm of love. The child's nurse works under rules and according to hours. The infant's mother has no employer to prescribe for her. Her time is her own. But is it? No, a mother's love knows no time schedule, no nights out, no days off. She carries her concern for her child into her very dreams. Her sleep is sensitive to the slightest need of the little one. The sky is the limit of a true mother's love.

The laws of friendship are not standardized.

No code of hours or pay can be worked out for comradeship. The friend does not have to obey rules as to how much time he will give or what service he is expected to render. But when a person is in trouble, what true friend ever thinks he is doing enough to help? Genuine friends gladly go "the second mile" and give "the cloak also." There are no upper limits of friendship. This is the reason for its beauty and its boundless demands. And this is the reason why Jesus raised his disciples from the status of servants to that of friends (John 15. 15).

In giving principles rather than rules Jesus took off the upper limits of what was expected of his followers. Making the methods of obedience less rigid, he made the demands more exacting. "How oft shall my brother sin against me, and I forgive him? Until seven times?" (Matthew 18. 21.) The rabbinical rule held that three times was expected. Peter, remembering that his Master had bidden their righteousness to exceed the righteousness of the scribes and Pharisees, went beyond the rabbinical requirement and suggested the sacred number seven in his question. But Jesus replied, "I say not unto thee, Until seven times; but, Until seventy times seven" (Matthew 18. 22).

Can we read such passages and say that Jesus in giving principles rather than rules toned down

the ethical requirements for his followers?   No.
We are not quite sure that we understand Reinhold Niebuhr's explanation of the optimistic
credo accepted by certain sections of liberal
Christianity when he writes, "It was aided in
doing this by the fortuitous circumstances that the
impossibility of an impossible possibility was implicit rather than explicit in the thought of
Jesus."[6]   But we do agree with Niebuhr's contention that Jesus' commands to love may be called
an "impossible possibility" and as such relevant
to our present ethical situations.   His thought
was not on the compromises of a worldly life. The
way of Jesus may still be higher than our ways as
"the heavens are higher than the earth," but just
as we earth-bound creatures are more and more
penetrating and utilizing the heavens, so we convention-bound men may make increasing contact
between our "practical" ethics and the principles
of Jesus.

----

[6] Reinhold Niebuhr, *An Interpretation of Christian Ethics*,
p. 119. Harper and Brothers, New York.

CHAPTER III

THE REASONS FOR THE UNREASONABLE

SINCE we cannot dismiss the difficult and puzzling statements of Jesus by these easy methods which we have discussed, let us now see if we can peer into the purpose which lay behind the paradoxes of Jesus.

We have already suggested one practical reason for the Master's use of paradox. He attracted and riveted attention to his principles by putting them into paradoxes rather than into detailed codes and conventional prose. It has been whimsically remarked that a paradox is a truth standing on its head to attract attention. We can hardly think of Jesus deliberately resorting to literary acrobatics and legerdemain in order to catch the public eye after the fashion of a Chesterton or Bernard Shaw. But he was a pioneer and a poet, and in both capacities he found paradox a legitimate and effective device for illuminating neglected aspects of truth and opening new paths of thought. By its seeming self-contradiction a paradox challenges sluggish minds, by its apparent absurdity it provokes that skepticism which is the matrix of study. and by touching the nerve of surprise it stimulates fresh insights.

But Jesus was prompted to the use of paradox by a second concern, deeper than the mere desire to make his utterances striking and memorable. He had to show that the discovery of his spiritual truths requires more than secular knowledge. When his own Galilean neighbors were turning from him in disbelief, he exclaimed,"I thank thee, O Father, Lord of heaven and earth, that thou didst hide these things from the wise and understanding, and didst reveal them unto babes" (Matthew 11. 25). In such utterance Jesus was not discounting the use of reason, but he was reflecting on its proneness to self-deceit. "We must admit, in sober sadness, that the intellect too brings its temptations, that the man who reasons is prone to deceive himself, that science has a tendency to close the mind in a narrow circle of self-complacency, and that the professed agnostic is peculiarly liable to a callous conceit. Such, we know, was the discovery of Socrates, when he set out on his search for the wise man, and found everywhere, and most prominently there where reputation for wisdom was greatest, that men thought they knew what they did not know at all." [1] What Socrates discovered under the por-

---

[1] Paul Elmer More, *The Christ of the New Testament*, p. 102. Princeton University Press.

ticoes of Athens, Jesus rediscovered among the scribes of Palestine. John Galsworthy called attention to the same tendency in what he quite originally termed "the cock-eyed cocksureness of writers."

The Master realized that he could not expound his principles by lectures nor save men by discussion. Hence his short and cryptic answers to Nicodemus and to Pilate. Jesus was not a demonstrator for spectators but a sower going forth to sow. His parables and paradoxes were kernels of truth which had to germinate in congenial soil. Hence it was in the receptive spirits and fertile imaginations of childlike minds that the paradoxical epigrams of Jesus could unfold themselves and take root.

Jesus addressed his little band of disciples as if it were a secret society, whose passwords could not be given to the uninitiated. "Unto you is given the mystery of the kingdom of God: but unto them that are without, all things are done in parables: that seeing they may see, and not perceive; and hearing they may hear, and not understand; lest haply they should turn again, and it should be forgiven them" (Mark 4. 11, 12). It is worse than futile to try to rationalize the deep inner formulas of Jesus for the casual bystanders and the merely intellectually curious. Initiation into the spirit of his company must precede interpretation of the secrets of his teaching.

For this reason Jesus chose a small group of followers to live with him until they could become the understanding custodians of Kingdom mysteries hidden from the "wise" outsiders. His spirit had to be caught before it could be taught. The fourth Gospel gives an insight into this teaching technique of Jesus. When two followers of John the Baptist beheld the Nazarene newcomer, they were so fascinated that they started to follow him. Jesus, seeing that they were pursuing, turned and asked, "What seek ye?" They countered with a question, "Rabbi, . . . where abidest thou?" Jesus replied, "Come, and ye shall see" (John 1. 37, 39). However difficult it may be to reconcile that incident with the Synoptic chronology, it does fit into the method of the Master. The first followers of Jesus were won not by argument, but by living contact. They were to "come and see," to take up a cross and follow him. In the laboratory of Jesus experience preceded explanation.

The requirement of spiritual surrender before intellectual illumination was no more abitrary than the attitude of any good physician. Suppose a person were to approach a doctor in the eclectic spirit with which Nicodemus or the Sadducees came to question Jesus. The caller speaks somewhat as follows: "Doctor, I realize there is something wrong with my condition, and I am consulting various physicians around the city in the hope that out of their combined diagnoses and prescriptions I can find the cure for my ailment." Would a respectable medical man take a patient on such a basis? Decidedly not. He would tell his caller to go to some other doctor's office—or perhaps some place less comfortable. A good physician requires his patient to submit himself to his regimen and give it a wholehearted, undivided trial. A competent doctor does not try to explain his cure to the "wise" spectator; he demonstrates it to the willing patient.

Professor Eddington, of Cambridge, has discussed with delightful sarcasm the folly of trying to rationalize religious formulas in advance of personal experience. He uses this analogy from the physical world: "I am standing on the threshold about to enter a room. It is a complicated business. In the first place I must shove against an atmosphere pressing with a force of fourteen pounds on every square inch of my body. I must make sure of landing on a plank traveling at twenty miles a second round the sun. . . . I must do this while hanging from a round planet, head outward into space, and with a wind of ether blowing at no one knows how many miles a second through every interstice of my body. The plank has no solidity of substance. To step on it is like stepping on a swarm of flies. Shall I not slip through? . . . Verily, it is easier for a camel to pass through the eye of a needle than for a scientific man to pass through a door. And whether the door be a barn door or a church door, it might be wiser that he should consent to be an ordinary man and walk in rather than wait until all the difficulties involved in a really scientific ingress are resolved."[2]

Likewise, entrance into the kingdom of heaven cannot be mapped and reasoned in advance. "To them that are without, all things are done in parables."

A third reason for the use of paradox is that the mysteries of human life elude the grasp of scientific knowledge even when it humbly and earnestly seeks. The three recognized steps by which science proceeds are classification, analysis, and explanation. Now, a human being may be classified according to his race, his nationality, his personality, his temperament, or a dozen other categories of description. We can partly analyze him into his physiological and psychological elements. We can partially explain his conduct and career by heredity and environment. But all these fall far short of comprehending the individuality of a person. Alexis Carrel, distinguished spokes-

[2] A. S. Eddington, *The Nature of the Physical World*, p. 342. 1929. The Macmillan Company, New York.

man of science, reveals how limited is the knowledge of personality in the title of his recent book, *Man, the Unknown.*

Even physiologically every man has individual differences. Each finger tip, each ear, has an individuality all its own. Strictly speaking, every human body is "in a class by itself." And as to personality, that transcends scientific analysis still more. "It frequently happens that a patient with whom one physician can do nothing is easily cured by another practitioner, who, generally speaking, is in no way his superior, simply because the one has, and the other has not, a temperament sympathetic to this particular patient."[3] This difference in healing power of two men equally equipped is one of the mysteries of personality which are hidden from the "wise and understanding."

Some twenty years ago a certain man held a preaching fellowship in one of our leading theological seminaries. He had finished the undergraduate courses with such proficiency that he had been kept on for further work in the art of preaching. Today he is lost on one of the lower rungs of mediocrity in the ministry. Recently one of his former teachers, speaking of this man, said: "He ought to be a good preacher. He

---

[3] B. H. Streeter, *Reality*, p. 105. The Macmillan Company, New York.

has all the requirements, except that essential something, that necessary spark." The presence or absence of that necessary spark is another of the mysteries of life which are hidden from "the wise and understanding."

Twenty-five years ago a husband was taking his frail little wife on a sea voyage for her health. On that trip he was suddenly stricken by death and was buried at sea. That woman, who hitherto had been supported by her strong stalwart husband, returned to take up the responsibilities of her large family and wide interests. In doing so she developed a tireless energy and executive efficiency which were the marvel of all who knew her. Her resources of strength were another one of those mysteries which are hidden from "the wise and understanding," for therein was revealed that which is "able to do exceeding abundantly above all that we ask or think, according to the power that worketh in us."

Not only does human life have these margins which extend beyond rational or scientific explanation, but it often seems to run counter to reason and logic. Reason would warrant the expectation that joy should inspire the singer's most beautiful strains, yet "our sweetest songs are those which tell of saddest thought." Logic would lead to the assumption that material comfort should breed the strongest confidence in God's goodness, but history reveals that our prosperous periods and groups produce the most religious skepticism. Our most pessimistic modern writing is wafted down from penthouses while our most optimistic utterances rise from pioneers on rough frontiers. Reason would prompt the conclusion that, since shoes and clothes which fit give comfort, therefore man would be most happy when everything in his environment had been shaped to fit him; but human nature seems adjusted to maladjustment and men find their maximum happiness struggling against obstacles.

Life is larger than logic. "It looks just a little more mathematical and regular than it is; its exactitude is obvious, but its inexactitude is hidden; its wildness lies in wait."[4] Those aspects of life which cannot be caught by the camera of logic or analyzed in the dissecting room of science—those require the method of paradox for their expression.

Hence Jesus made use of paradox as a means of dealing with the suprarational elements of life. He "put to shame them that are wise" by outdistancing their worldly wisdom. Jesus did not outrage reason; he outran it. He exceeded the wisdom of the knowing ones as the old bishop shocked the judgment of his housekeeper in giving to Jean Valjean the other candlestick. His

[4] G. K. Chesterton, *Orthodoxy*, p. 148. John Lane & Company.

was not a blind faith. It was a seeing faith, seeing more than the others saw. Jesus outtrusted the wise. "He put to shame them that are wise" as a certain wife shamed the wisdom of her friends when a few years ago she seemed to have exhausted all reasonable means of reforming her husband. He appeared to be completely washed out. But she still believed there was a vein of gold in him and she continued to prospect on his promises. Her acquaintances said it was only another case of love being blind. But was her love blind or did it see what others missed? At any rate she has now restored her home to happiness.

Jesus, in using parables and paradoxes, outran the rational as Charles Dodgson outran the science of mathematics when, as Lewis Carroll, he wrote *Alice's Adventures in Wonderland.* The Oxford don, like the Nazarene Carpenter, was trying to tell us that the world is a wonderland which cannot be charted completely by the instruments of science. Our codified knowledge is but a little island in the boundless ocean of mystery. The larger the island grows, the longer the shoreline of mystery becomes.

The paradoxes of Jesus serve both as reminders of the limitations of logic and as incentives to explore beyond them. They are like Browning's "paradox that comforts while it mocks."

CHAPTER IV

THE CONSERVATIVE REVOLUTIONARY

WHEN Peter delivered his sermon from Solomon's porch, he characterized Jesus in words translated by the King James Version as "the Prince of life." Moffatt makes it read "the pioneer of Life." Each seems a legitimate interpretation of the Greek, but the words suggest almost opposite aspects of activity. "Prince" suggests rich background and royal ancestry. "Pioneer" connotes humble beginnings and long foreground.

Nevertheless, both terms fit the figure of Jesus. He was the heir of Israel's royal hopes. He allowed himself to be regarded as the fulfillment of her Messianic prophecies. He began his public ministry by asserting his continuity with the religious life of his countrymen through the baptism of John. In his first recorded synagogue appearance at Nazareth he read from one of Isaiah's Messianic prophecies and then concluded by saying, "Today hath this scripture been fulfilled in your ears" (Luke 4. 21). In the light of Jesus' actions and utterances John Macmurray has much justification in saying, "Jesus offered himself to his people from the first as the Messiah of the Old Testament prophecies."[1]

Whether we agree with the statement that Jesus openly "offered himself . . . as the Messiah," we must recognize that his use of the expression "Son of man" would arouse Messianic expectations. The phrase was a bit ambiguous, but it stemmed from the traditional hopes of Israel's recovered glory. Jesus was looked upon as the longed-for leader of restoration. He seemed to encourage that view of himself. "Think not that I am come to destroy the law or the prophets; I came not to destroy but to fulfill. For verily I say unto you, Till heaven and earth pass away, one jot or one tittle shall in no wise pass from the law, till all things be fulfilled" (Matthew 5. 17, 18). Jesus of Nazareth, descended from David's line, appeared as the Prince of life, the Preserver of the law and the prophets.

On the other hand, Jesus cut loose from the positions of Israel's lawmakers with the daring of a pioneer. Boldly and repeatedly he asserted, "Ye have heard that it was said to them of old time, Thou shalt not kill; and whosoever shall kill shall be in danger of the judgment: but I say unto you, that every one who is angry with his brother shall be in danger of the judgment; and whosoever shall say to his brother, Raca, shall be in danger of the

[1] John Macmurray, *Creative Society*, p. 52. Eddy and Page.

council; and whosoever shall say, Thou fool, shall be in danger of the hell of fire" (Matthew 5. 21, 22). "Ye have heard that it was said, Thou shalt not commit adultery: but I say unto you, that every one that looketh on a woman to lust after her hath committed adultery with her already in his heart" (Matthew 5. 27, 28). "It was said also, Whosoever shall put away his wife, let him give her a writing of divorcement: but I say unto you, that every one that putteth away his wife, saving for the cause of fornication, maketh her an adulteress: and whosoever shall marry her when she is put away committeth adultery" (Matthew 5. 31, 32). He assumed authority to lay down new principles of action. He strove to disabuse men's minds of the belief that he was merely putting new patches on the torn garments of old laws. Unlike John the Baptist, Jesus and his disciples discarded some of the fasts and ceremonials observed by the Pharisees, for his new wine was not to be poured into old bottles. (Matthew 9. 17.) His kingdom was not to come by a process of mending the old order. Nothing less than a new birth would give entrance to the society which Jesus heralded.

There was a surgical sharpness about Jesus' severance from the old traditions. "Leave the dead to bury their own dead" (Luke 9. 60) was his enigmatical counsel to the would-be disciple who wanted to return to his father's house; and it had a wider application than to the individual directly concerned. "No man, having put his hand to the plough, and looking back, is fit for the kingdom of God" (Luke 9. 62). "Eyes front" is the command of Jesus, the Pioneer of life. He knew that the suction of what is behind is a greater deterrent than the resistance of what is ahead—a truth recently recognized in our physical realm by our automotive engineers, who now construct our cars with obtuse front and tapering rear.

Yet Jesus was no ruthless iconoclast. He possessed a historical perspective which made progress toward the new by keeping track of the past. As the chauffeur's mirror on a modern car enables the driver to see what is behind without taking his major gaze from the road ahead, so Jesus kept in view the old laws of Israel in order that he might make better headway toward the new laws of the kingdom of heaven. For, significantly enough, it is when we would turn left that we most need to see the road behind us. Likewise, in our social progress it is our "left" turns which need to be safeguarded by historical perspective lest in trying to move toward the new we be run into by some old error coming down the road bearing a modern license plate.

It was this consciousness of the past which made Jesus a more genuine conservative than the scribes and Pharisees themselves. The latter were obscuring the original fundamental religious laws and values by their accretions of ceremony and tradition. "Ye leave the commandment of God, and hold fast the tradition of men" (Mark 7. 8, 9). Jesus pruned away these dead limbs which bore no fruit, thereby helping to preserve the body of the law.

It was also this clear historical perspective of Jesus which made him more patient than John the Baptist in method and yet more radical in motive. The impetuous forerunner announced, "And even now the ax lieth at the root of the trees: every tree therefore that bringeth not forth good fruit is hewn down, and cast into the fire" (Matthew 3. 10). But Jesus did not talk about laying axes at the roots of trees. He did on one occasion liken himself to a gardener standing before a barren fig tree, asking for more time to dig around it, that he might make it bear fruit (Luke 13. 6-9). John the Baptist expected the Messiah to come with an ax to cut out, but Jesus came with a spade to make grow.

But while the spade seems gentler and less radical than the ax, nevertheless Jesus' program was much more revolutionary than John's. When the Baptist's hearers asked, "What shall we do then?" John replied, "He that hath two coats. let him impart to him that hath none; and he that hath food, let him do likewise. . . . Extort no more than that which is appointed you. . . . Extort from no man by violence, neither accuse *any one* wrongfully; and be content with your wages" (Luke 3. 10-14). What tame, half-way prescriptions are these in comparison with the new commands of Jesus:—"And if any man would go to law with thee, and take away thy coat, let him have thy cloak also" (Matthew 5. 40). "Sell whatsoever thou hast, and give to the poor, and thou shalt have treasure in heaven" (Mark 10. 21). "Whosoever smiteth thee on thy right cheek, turn to him the other also" (Matthew 5. 39). "Love your enemies, and pray for them that persecute you" (Matthew 5. 44). Yes, the spade of Jesus goes far deeper than the ax of John.

Jesus, the Gardener of God, came into a wilderness of legalism with the creative spirit of a true pioneer. He cut away the secondary growths of convention and tradition that he might renew the primary roots of life's laws. Thus he slashed away the underbrush of overlying restrictions and laid bare the first and great commandment of love to God and the second, like unto it, of love to neighbor. "On these two commandments," he said, "hangeth the whole law and the prophets" (Matthew 22. 40). Such a radical reduction of laws was sufficient in itself to be called revolutionary.

And then Jesus proceeded to take those two

central roots of love to God and neighbor and transplant them into new spheres of application. "Who is my neighbor?" asked the scribe to whom the law had just been laid down. For answer, Jesus told the parable of the good Samaritan, a story which stretches the limit of brotherhood beyond the old nationalistic and racial boundaries. He gave a new conception of community universal in reach. He reduced in order to expand.

Not only did Jesus universalize the essential laws of Judaism, but he also spiritualized them. In his wilderness temptation he repudiated the traditional reliance on physical force as the way of establishing the Messianic kingdom. And in his cleansing of the Temple he boldly reasserted his desire to deliver the faith of his fathers from its blighting materialism. His was a morality of inwardness and conscience. His way to the Kingdom was not by external revolution but by internal regeneration. This reliance on regeneration rather than revolution was in itself too revolutionary for the mass of his followers. They deserted him. Jesus was left to his crucifiers because he was too spiritually radical for the revolutionists.

How new was Jesus? Much discussion has been given to the question of his originality.[2] The

[2] H. R. Mackintosh, *The Originality of the Christian Message.* Duckworth and Co.

parallels to his precepts have been traced through Hebrew and Greek sources. Some see the genius of Jesus chiefly in his poetic power of packing beauty and truth into crisp epigram and lovely parable. They find his originality in the form rather than the substance of his doctrine. Others think his uniqueness lies in the scope of his vision and his profound insight into the conditions demanded for its accomplishment. But must we not thoughtfully seek the chief originality of Jesus on a level deeper than that of literary form or mental insight?

"It is the spirit that quickeneth; the flesh profiteth nothing: the words that I have spoken unto you are spirit, and are life" (John 6. 63). His words had a kindling power of stirring others to original effort. They set his followers to asking and seeking and knocking and finding. They stirred liberating spirits out of the chrysalis of their complacency and sent them winging their way toward new adventures. They took hold of convention-bound conservatives and caused them to try the second mile and turn the other cheek. There was something about the Carpenter from the hill country which could lead four fishermen to launch out from a comfortable livelihood into the financially uncertain business of fishing for men. It was something deeper than a question of how new Jesus was. It was his power to inspire

newness of life in others. Beyond any question
the most distinguishing mark of Jesus' originality
was that he made for the originality of his followers.

There was a note of revolutionary daring about
this which has been lost sight of in our contemporary Christianity. A young college woman
some time ago passed a trenchant criticism on the
conventional sermon. She said that no matter
where a preacher started into his discourse, one
always knew where he was coming out—which,
by the way, is more than many ministers themselves seem to know; that however dark the picture painted at the beginning, the conclusion
always was that Christ would bring things out
right in the end. No doubt that is the impression
given by our usual sermonizing. Our proclaiming of the Christian message resembles the presen-
tation of a familiar Shakespearian plot in that we
know how it is coming out. But that is exactly
what was not the case with the original gospel of
Christ. Those first followers of Jesus did not
know how it was coming out. Therein lies the
glory of their going forth.

Jesus was a pioneer with no earthly precedent
to guide him. He was the leader of a revolution
without historical pattern. He held before men
the prospectus of the kingdom of heaven. He
lured his followers with the promise of perfection.

He was the pursuer of a flying goal. By being more spiritually radical than the social revolutionists of his day he lost his own life, but he kept alive "the law and the prophets." He was the Conservative Revolutionary.

CHAPTER V

THE GOOD TEMPTER

SOME years ago a sincere layman complained that men came to church in order to get help for their burdens and temptations, but the ministers, instead of aiding in solving those problems which the people brought, only added to their confusion by creating new puzzles and questions. The gentleman's position does appear to deserve some sympathy. Harassed and hard-driven human beings have a right to expect help from their religious teachers in meeting the difficulties which they bring with them to their places of worship. Nevertheless, if this were all that the Christian Church does for men, it would hardly be up to the standard set by its Founder.

For Jesus was more a creator of questions than a quieter of minds. Or rather, it might be said that his way of quieting minds was by creating questions. This paradoxical principle was basic to his general program of helping and healing. He was the Burden-Bearer who offered tired men a yoke. He was the Physician who healed sick spirits with a cross. He was the Saviour who rescued the tempted by leading them into new temptations.

Jesus was first of all a teacher. And poor indeed as an educator would be the teacher who only helped the pupils with the problems and questions which they brought to school. Far short of his high functions as a disciplinarian would be the teacher who considered his task to be only that of aiding his charges in overcoming temptations which they knew they had.

No, the good teacher arouses new questions in his pupils' minds as well as helps to answer their old ones. A good school lures its students with good temptations toward larger horizons and loftier truths. The teacher of English tries to tempt the youth's taste for good literature by introducing him to the stately cadences of a Milton and the scintillating insights of a Shakespeare. The teacher of art essays to arouse the hunger for beauty by leading the student into the mellowing presence of a Sistine Madonna, or showing him the canvas of a Corot with the sunlight streaming through the gnarled branches of a tree. The instructor in history endeavors to fire the mind of the modern boy with the glowing figures of the past so that the lad may feel like the young Greek who, after pondering his ancestors' achievements, cried, "The trophies of Miltiades will not let me sleep."

Thus, education rightly managed, is a succession of good temptations, upward, outward, onward.

And Jesus, being a teacher, worked on that principle. He did not strive merely to help men resist their forbidden desires. When Odysseus and his sailors came near the island of the sirens and heard the seductive music wooing them toward the shore, Odysseus stuffed their ears to shut out the tempting strains. But when Orpheus and his crew sailed past the dangerous isle, he took out his lyre and struck up a sweeter melody so that the sirens' voices were no longer heard.

Jesus proceeded on the principle of Orpheus rather than Odysseus. He did not bid his followers to stop their ears and blind their eyes to things of earth. Rather he unstopped the ears of the deaf and opened the eyes of the blind that they might hear and see the better things to the ignoring of the bad. True, he did give some sharp, penetrating commands about plucking out the lustful eye and cutting off the offending hand. The white armor of his purity could tolerate no stain of evil. No reformer ever cut so deeply into the quick of sinful desire. Yet Jesus had no sin obsession. He was a purist, but he did not give the impression of a Puritanical crusader. The Master's way was to overcome evil with good. He saw that the cure for low appetites was the awakening of higher hungers, that the prevention of the ugly and the vulgar lies in cultivating a taste for the beautiful and the genuine.

This Galilean principle explains why Jesus gave so much more effort to arousing the respectable people of Palestine than to restraining the disreputable. It is significant to note how little space the Gospels give to denouncing the out-and-out flagrant physical vices and how much they devote to the subtle sins of the respectable.

For example, there was highway robbery in Jesus' day, but he did not say much about that crime. Oh, to be sure, he told the story of a man who fell among robbers on the Jericho road, but the point of the parable of the good Samaritan was not to denounce the dangers of crime on the highway. It was, rather, to arouse the respectable priests and Levites toward a more sympathetic type of neighborliness.

Also, first-century Palestine had its dens of vice. The Master makes mention of a young fellow who left his father's house and fell into licentious living. But the story of the prodigal son does not dwell long on the lurid scenes of that country. One can imagine what a modern scenario writer for a Hollywood studio would do with such a setting. But Jesus just gave a thumb-nail sketch of the vice dens in passing on to the main point of that immortal parable, which was the warm fatherly love thawing out the icicled springs of the cold elder brother.

This focusing of effort on the mental sins of

the respectable rather than on the crude vices of the body does not mean that Jesus condoned the bestial physical sins. No, not that. But our bodily vices have a way of begetting their own punishment and prevention. Lust brings the disordered life and the disreputable career. Drunkenness leaves the bleary eye and the weakened frame. Our physical evils tend eventually to advertise themselves openly. But the sins of the mind are so much more subtly dangerous because they conceal themselves, often even from their possessor. That explains the Master's statement to the chief priests and elders, "The publicans and the harlots go into the kingdom of God before you" (Matthew 21. 31). And in his pictures of the final Judgment the grounds of condemnation are not the sordid and vicious violations of the moral code but the sins of inattention and inconsiderateness. Dives had not concerned himself about the beggar at his gate. "Inasmuch as ye did it not unto one of these least, ye did it not unto me. And these shall go away into eternal punishment" (Matthew 25. 45-46). Jesus did not need to spend time in denouncing the obvious sins of the publicans and harlots. His major effort was to awaken so-called good people to discover the shortcomings which they did not know they had.

Let us watch the Galilean in one or two of his cases. Take Nathanael, for example. The record says that Nathanael was "an Israelite indeed, in whom is no guile!" (John 1. 47.) His mind lay like the limpid waters of a little lake, clear all the way to the bottom. He appeared free from all moral deceit. But when he heard of Jesus' redemptive mission, Nathanael exclaimed, "Can any good thing come out of Nazareth?" Ah, there is revealed the hidden sin of Nathanael. He was narrow-minded. He could not believe high expectations coming from a neighboring town which he looked down upon. Now, narrow-mindedness is a sin which a man may have for years without knowing it. For the moment a man admits that he is narrow-minded, he is beginning to broaden.

Jesus came to make the narrow-minded Nathanaels aware of their subtle sin and to broaden their horizons toward the brotherhood of the kingdom of God, which outruns the boundaries of race, color, or creed. And if we are inclined to regard narrowness as not a very serious sin, we might remind ourselves that a powerful, narrow-minded man who does not share the interests and needs of his fellow men can do more damage than a dozen drunken derelicts.

Or turn to the case of Peter. Peter was a fisherman, and that is a vocation which has its peculiar temptations. Fishermen have a temptation to impatience when they fish long and take little.

Also they often seem to have a temptation to profanity when they make a catch and then lose it. Moreover, many fishermen succumb to the temptation to prevarication, or at least exaggeration, in reporting their successes. Peter, apparently, was subject to all three of these sets of temptations. But Jesus did not merely talk to Peter about overcoming his impatience, his profanity, and his boasting. No, Jesus said, "Come, and I will make you a fisher of men." That is, the Master gave Peter a whole new conception of his life's work. He raised his purpose from the level of material values to the plane of human values.

Consider also what Jesus did for Zacchaeus. That publican was well aware of his temptation to false accusation and his sin of dishonesty. But at the dinner table that day in Jericho he had his eyes opened to a shortcoming hitherto hidden from himself. Zacchaeus was so obsessed with the social coldness toward himself that he did not realize how hard his own nature had become. As he met the gaze of his Galilean Guest, he was stung by the thought of his own stinginess and hardheartedness. And he came forth to announce that the half of his goods he would give to the poor. Hardheartedness, like narrow-mindedness, is one of those sins to which we have to be awakened.

Or watch the Master in one more case, that of the woman who came to the Samaritan well. That woman was in a sullen and rebellious mood. Decent society had shut its doors against her and she had shut the doors of her life against decency. As we would say, she felt "sunk." She was down and almost out. Now, a person knows when he is "sunk," for then everything around seems to rise to undue proportions. Molehill troubles loom as mountains and we seem as grasshoppers in the midst of giants.

But when Jesus began to talk to that woman about a well of water, deep down in her nature, which could spring up into eternal life, he revealed to her a sin which she did not know she had, namely, that of shallowness. Her life had filled up with sediment until she had grown shallow. She was trying to draw her satisfactions from superficial and artificial sources. The deep artesian springs of her own nature had dried up. And while a person knows when he is "sunk," he does not know when he is shallow. Surface living is an unhealthy condition, so deceptively satisfying that one has to be stirred out of it by some experience wherein "deep calleth unto deep." And that is one of Jesus' good temptations.

He came to tempt men from the shallows into the deeps, from narrowness into brotherhood, from crowd morality into a righteousness that exceeds, from the quiescence of unconcern into the "peace of God which passeth all understanding."

As a modern writer has put it, Jesus of Nazareth was a mighty moral huntsman, sweeping across the landscape of history, digging men out of the little burrows of respectability in which they had ensconced themselves.

CHAPTER VI

THE TOLERANT DICTATOR

WHEN Dwight L. Moody was conducting his revival campaigns a half century ago, he organized bands of personal workers who went back into the congregation and accosted friends or even strangers with the question, "What will you do with Jesus?" That was an accepted method of evangelism which continued down to days remembered by many of us. Such a practice would now, however, arouse resentment in most circles wherein we move. The man on the street, and certainly the man on the campus, would be disposed to meet the question, "What will you do with Jesus?" with an answering query, "Why do I have to do anything with Jesus?"

To meet this modern mood the Church has made a marked change in its method of presenting Jesus. Once it stationed itself at the gates of the world somewhat as the trainman stands at the gates of a railroad station, asking passengers to show their tickets. The Church stood at the entrance of birth and asked children to show a baptismal certificate or else the little passengers traveled at their own risk of eternal damnation. Not so long ago, missionary leaders would stand in our pulpits with their watches in hand asserting that at every tick so many heathen were departing for perdition because the gospel of Christ had not reached them. Thus the Church stood at the exit of death and claimed the power to pass on a man's ticket for eternity. If the departing traveler had not received the ecclesiastical blessing and pardon, he was regarded as headed for darkness.

Now we of the Protestant fold, at least, would hardly presume to separate the sheep from the goats in such definite fashion. We recognize that there are men who, like John Stuart Mill, may be unable to subscribe to the creed of a church and yet do spend themselves in Christian spirit for the welfare of their fellow men. We think of George Eliot with all her religious doubts, writing in her *Romola* one of the most moving studies of the atonement. We would be loath to claim that church membership is the criterion by which eternal welfare is to be determined.

Our old churchyards are sometimes silent reminders of the lines drawn by our forefathers. Ellen Glasgow, in her *Vein of Iron*, makes much of the murderer's grave outside the burial ground and of the Magdalene's hovel outside the village. The minister who himself had felt the excommunicating power of the early Calvinistic group explained the situation. He said: "If they turned her out of the church, it is scarcely logical to expect them to welcome her in the churchyard. Dead Presbyterians are still Presbyterians, only more so."

Today the Protestant Church stands, not like the trainman at the gate asking passengers to show their tickets, but more like the attendants at the Information Bureau or the Travelers' Aid desk. We of the ministry do not halt men with our authoritative questions. Rather we stand ready to serve those who come to us with their questions. In medieval times the Church stood out in the center of European traffic with the manner of the uniformed officer empowered to start and stop. In modern times our churches stand back of the sidewalk asking the privilege of helping.

Ours is a day of electives in college and eclecticism in thought. Our expanding horizons embrace the domains of non-Christian religions and we make comparative studies of their claims.

The most representative ambassadors of Christianity to the mission field go in the spirit of sharing, not of competing. They use their medical and surgical skill to save the lives of Orientals whether they be Buddhists or Shintoists. They employ their improved agricultural methods to provide food for the undernourished whether they be followers of Confucius or Mohammed. If our Christian contacts can bestir non-Christian cultures to better health and higher standards, we rejoice.

In our modern mood of intellectual independence it seems an unwarrantable presumption to present Jesus of Nazareth as a figure for or against whom we have to make a decision.

Yet, when we go back to the New Testament, we find his followers asserting the claim that Jesus Christ controls the entrances to salvation. Peter, in his powerful defense delivered before Annas and Caiaphas, boldly asserted: "In none other is there salvation: for neither is there any other name under heaven, that is given among men, wherein we must be saved" (Acts 4. 12). In the fourth Gospel, we read that Jesus made similar claims for himself. "I am the way, and the truth, and the life: no one cometh unto the Father but by me" (John 14. 6). And even if we allow for elaboration and coloration in such passages, the Synoptic Gospels show us a personality who challenged mankind with the arresting assertion that no one could be neutral toward him. "He that is not with me is against me" (Luke 11. 23). *dictator*

That statement in itself seems almost a paradox. Is it not absurd for any person to say that others have to take a stand either for or against him? And the paradox is heightened by another assertion standing just ahead of it: "He that is not against us is for us" (Mark 9. 40) Both statements seem *Tolerance* too inclusive in their claim, and yet each seems to exclude the other. On the face of it the former appears to force men into narrow sectarianism; the latter seems to open the way for broad tolerance.

Let us look for light to the occasions which called forth these utterances. In the ninth chapter of Mark and in the ninth chapter of Luke is recorded the incident of John coming to Jesus and saying: "We saw one casting out demons in thy name: and we forbade him, because he followed not us." To this Jesus replied, "Forbid him not . . . for he that is not against us is for us." Here speaks the voice of tolerance. Jesus would not restrain the other healer because he did not carry his label and join his company. The Great Physician was concerned with the good accomplished and not with the credit received. Any worker who was genuinely bringing health to men was engaged in the Kingdom enterprise which Jesus came to establish. The common worthy object made the workers comrades regardless of company formations.

Jesus' attitude toward the other healer was an expression of the broad spirit characteristic of him. He was so charitable in his judgments of men. He warned his followers against impugning the motives of others. "Judge not, that ye be not judged" (Matthew 7. 1). Jesus ridiculed those

censorious folk who went about in his day looking for the motes in others' eyes. There was none
of the narrowness of fanaticism about the Man of
Nazareth who dined with Pharisees and publicans,
who chose Samaritans as heroes for his parables
and paid high compliments to Roman centurions.
Jesus was free too from that impatience which so
frequently taints the crusader. He would not
rashly rush in to root out the tares, but with calm
confidence would await the sifting time of harvest
(compare Matthew 13. 24-30). While his avoidance of many current issues may be understood as
due to his singleness of spiritual purpose,
nevertheless, he did not display that single-track
intensity which characterizes the man of one idea.
Jesus saw life steadily, and he saw it whole.

Jesus did not dash up and down Palestine like
a modern crusader putting across a campaign. He
poured out his service in the broad inclusive spirit
of his Heavenly Father who "maketh his sun to
rise on the evil and the good, and sendeth rain on
the just and the unjust" (Matthew 5. 45). He
seemed to realize that the results of his work
would overflow far beyond the borders of any
church which might bear his name and any group
which would give him credit. If others, like the
contemporary healer, sought to rival the activities
of his own company, Jesus' principle was to surpass, not to suppress.

But how can we reconcile such genial tolerance
with Jesus' other assertion?—"He that is not with
me is against me; and he that gathereth not with
me scattereth" (Luke 11. 23). That seems tanta-
mount to saying that the person who is not the
friend of Jesus inevitably becomes his foe.

When we look at the situation which induced
this utterance, we find Jesus recorded as healing
a dumb man. The crowd standing by murmured
among themselves, saying that this ex-carpenter's
cures must be through the power of Beelzebub.
Jesus, divining their thoughts, answered them
with a shrewd bit of dialectic, ending with the
statement quoted above.

It is possible that many in that crowd were
priding themselves at the very moment on their
tolerance. They were skeptical of this new healer,
but they were not taking any steps to stop him.
They were not interfering with his work. They
were letting him go about his business. They were
merely neutral. But Jesus in substance told them
that they could not be strictly neutral toward him.
They were either with him or against him.

Consider a moment this matter of neutrality.
Suppose two friends of yours fall into a quarrel.
You decide to remain neutral. But how will you
preserve your neutrality? By refusing to assist
either of them, by being impartial in your attitude, by keeping completely out of the conflict?

If so, what will happen is that the stronger of the two will win his side of the issue. The neutrality of a third party inevitably works to the advantage of the stronger of the two contestants. You may neutralize your intentions but a policy of hands-off does not neutralize your influence. The weaker of the two could turn and say to you, "He that is not with me is against me."

Or turn from individuals to nations. In 1914 and 1915 the United States publicly reiterated its neutral position. But in reality our influence worked very one-sidedly. And finally we entered the war ostensibly in defense of our neutral rights. And in the recent conflict between Italy and Ethiopia we declared our neutrality by official act and proclamation. We pledged to prohibit the export of arms, ammunition, or implements of war to belligerent countries, to prohibit the transportation of war materials in American vessels, and to prohibit the travel of American passengers on the ships of belligerents during the war. Speaking broadly, we went about as far as a government can go in proclaiming a policy of "hands-off."

But while our intentions were impartial, our influence certainly was not. All that a powerful nation like Italy desired from her neighbors was that they stand aside while she carried out her purpose of subduing little Ethiopia. Such aloofness plays into the hands of the stronger contest-

ant. And Ethiopia would have been quite cor·
rect in saying to the United States or any other
government, "He that is not with me is against
me."

Similarly Jesus during his earthly career was in
conflict with the powerful, entrenched forces of a
corrupt social and religious regime. Whatever
the ultimately victorious divine power behind
him, he with his handful of followers was waging
an unequal contest. Therefore the neutral bystanders by their very passivity were giving aid to
his more powerful opponents. The professional
clique bent on putting Jesus out of the way
needed for its purpose nothing more than neutrality on the part of the public. Justified, therefore,
was Jesus in saying to the neutral crowd, "He that
is not with me is against me."

Herein he gave a necessary corrective to the
mistaken ideas of tolerance. Broad-mindedness
is a gracious virtue when genuine. But it has some
cheap counterfeits in circulation. There is a lot
of lazy thinking which passes current for broad-
mindedness. Indifference frequently masquerades
as tolerance. Many persons there are also who
think they are broad-minded when they are only
scatterbrained. Priding themselves on looking at
all sides of a situation, they get only a blurred
image of anything. Common too is that misuse
of Jesus' command of "Judge not," which creates

a clubbable atmosphere of mutual exoneration. When cowardice, compromise, unconcern, and neutrality cause a foggy thinking which is mistaken for tolerance, Jesus clears the air with his pertinent reminder, "He that is not with me is against me."

Then, according to Luke, Jesus adds a clause which expands this question of neutrality into a continuing and universalizing principle. "And he that gathereth not with me scattereth." Jesus is claiming to represent the gathering forces of life as opposed to the scattering forces. He is the rallying center of the world's routed army. His Kingdom principle is the centripetal force of the spiritual universe. This is the cosmic conception reflected by a follower who never saw Jesus in the flesh but who did feel his cohesive force permeating the world: "He is before all things, and in him all things hold together" (Colossians 1. 17).

The writer finds a homely observation making vivid this contrast between the centrifugal influences opposed to Jesus and the centripetal force represented in him. At Coney Island is an amusement device called the "human roulette wheel." The individual seeking his fun slides down an inclined plane and lands on a smoothly polished floor made up of contiguous revolving discs. The one on which he first lands whirls him about until it whisks him off on another which, in turn, spins him around until, the centrifugal forces having had their sport with him, he is deposited in disheveled state on the runway at the side. How symbolic of our social life is this Coney Island contrivance! A person rises in the morning. Before he leaves the modern home for his work, he is aware of the centrifugal individualism which has so largely whirled family units from the breakfast tables. Today each individual—for he usually eats alone—is the "autocrat of the breakfast table." He then goes forth into a daily routine made up of contacts with individuals and groups going around on the pivots of their own self-interest. He returns at night, bruised in spirit and dissipated in energy, hoping to pull himself together before he starts another day lest he entirely go to pieces. Such are the scattering forces of local living. The world shows the same set drawn to the scale of nations.

Below Niagara Falls there are many circles of whirling motion in the water of the river. Objects dropped into those whirlpools are not whisked off but drawn toward the center. The contrast between the centrifugal force of the spinning disc and the centripetal force of the whirlpool has suggested this difference: the former is revolving rigidly about its own center while the latter seems to be pouring itself at the center into something deeper. Whatever the relevancy of that observation to the scientific explanation, it does appear pertinent to human association. Whenever individuals or groups revolve on their own self-interests as center, they have a scattering effect. When they sink their interests into a deeper current of motivation, they have a gathering influence.

The Gospels present Jesus as the transformer of life's centrifugal forces into life's centripetal forces. By sinking self-interests into the current of the kingdom of God, the dissipating tendencies, such as fear, anxiety, and selfishness, are checked and the centralizing energies bring in the necessities of life. "Be not therefore anxious. . . . But seek ye first his kingdom, and his righteousness; and all these things shall be added unto you" (Matthew 6. 31, 33). Jesus is offered as the one who unifies the powers within the individual personality, who holds individuals together in groups, and who gathers group loyalties into a supreme centralizing loyalty. "In him all things hold together" (Colossians 1. 17).

The succeeding centuries have done much to substantiate that claim. Francis Thompson is the voice of experience when he describes the distracting and dissipating effects of his self-seeking, pleasure-loving existence until he heard and heeded the Voice which said, "All things betray thee who betrayest me." The individual who runs counter to Jesus' principles of living finds life running away from him.

When we turn from the individual to our social groupings, let us hear two men who spoke out of long experience in trying to co-ordinate the organizations of men. Henry George was one day talking with Cardinal Manning of their common interests. "I loved the people," he said, "and that love brought me to Christ as their best friend and teacher." The Cardinal replied, "And I loved Christ, and so learned to love the people for whom he died."[1] Manning, the churchman, by his contemplation of Christ was led to see that loyalty to him meant love for his fellow men. Henry George, the humanitarian, by his study of men's needs, came to realize that his love for his fellows led to loyalty to Christ.

Such is the testimony of the ages. Men group and regroup themselves around various centers of loyalty all the way from gangs to governments. But the processes of disintegration within groups and of destruction between groups keep society in continual turmoil, verging now toward chaos. Is there any centralizing power which can co-ordinate these conflicting loyalties? The New Testament says that there is. It is the power of the cosmic Christ, as pervasive, as pre-existent, as

Henry George, Jr., *Life of Henry George*, p. 438. Doubleday, Doran & Co.

inescapable as the force of gravity or as the energy of electricity.

Just as the electric energy was in the world before that day on which Franklin caught it on his key for the use of man, so the *Logos* was in the universe from the beginning, lighting every man coming into the world, and glimpsed in flashes by the founders of various religious faiths. But Jesus of Nazareth was that perfect personality which served as the Franklin key to bring the cosmic Christ to earth, where he could give men power to become the sons of God.

That is the Christian claim, implicit in the Synoptics and explicit in the fourth Gospel.

CHAPTER VII
THE STRICT LIBERATOR

ACCORDING to Luke, Jesus delivered what might be called his inaugural message in his home town of Nazareth. It was in the nature of an Emancipation Proclamation. The passage from Isaiah which he chose to read is keyed to the note of liberty.

"The spirit of the Lord is upon me,
Because he anointed me to preach good
  tidings to the poor:
He hath sent me to proclaim release to the cap-
  tives,
And recovering of sight to the blind,
To set at liberty them that are bruised,
To proclaim the acceptable year of the Lord"
  (Luke 4. 18, 19).

He explicitly announced that he had come to fulfill that prophecy (Luke 4. 21). He set forth in the rôle of a liberator, loosening the bodies of men from the grip of disease, freeing their minds from the shadows of fear, unshackling their wills from the bondage of sinful habit. While he did not give himself to social programs of civic and economic reform, he did impart the leavening spirit of liberty which was eventually to lift the status of the poor and the oppressed.

Jesus cut through the meshwork of legalistic restrictions which bound contemporary Judaism when he asserted that the whole law and the prophets hang on two single great commandments: "Thou shalt love the Lord thy God with all thy heart, and with all thy soul, . . . and with all thy mind;" and "Thou shalt love thy neighbor as thyself." Similarly, he proclaimed man's freedom from the burdensome institutionalism which ringed him round with custom. "The sabbath was made for man, and not man for the sabbath" (Mark 2. 27).

He sought to start the inner springs of spontaneous creative life in men. It was the fresh spontaneity of little children which he repeatedly held up as the requirement for entrance into the kingdom of heaven. When he was interviewed by a Nicodemus, careful for his reputation and cautious in his search for truth, Jesus called attention to the freedom of the wind which bloweth where it listeth. Not to weathervane minds, veering with the currents of popular opinion, could Jesus' secret be given, but to those who were willing to cut loose from the moorings of worldly position and go with the wind of the Spirit. In short, the adult seeker of the Kingdom must be born again into the unfettered imaginativeness and truthfulness and expectancy of childhood.

By his bearing even more than by explicit statement, Jesus carried an atmosphere of freedom. He was poorer than the foxes of the field and the fowls of the air, for he had "not where to lay his head" (Matthew 8. 20). Yet there was about him something of that carefree freedom which characterized those creatures. He was a carpenter carrying no purse of his own, yet when he passed the booth of Levi, the money-making publican, he had the liberating effect of a spring zephyr blowing over an imprisoned chrysalis, and ere long Levi became restless to wing his way out into the larger liberty of Jesus' way of life. Though poor, Jesus never gave the impression of being poverty-stricken. Though possessed of none of what men call "the good things of life," he so rose above the limitations of circumstance and made such a rich thing of living that a young scion of wealth came seeking his secret.

Caught at last in the clutches of his crucifiers, he did not look trapped and helpless. The disciple who betrayed him seemed to feel that Jesus was free to save himself if he would. The fourth Gospel reveals the impression made on his followers when it interprets Jesus as saying: "I lay down my life, that I may take it again. No one taketh it away from me, but I lay it down of myself" (John 10. 17, 18). And when he stood before Pilate at his trial, he seems restrained by an inner compul-

sion rather than by the power of the Roman law
or the Jewish mob. From the beginning to the
end of his public career he appeared to breathe
the air of freedom.

But, paradoxically, Jesus the Emancipator left
certain sayings which seem anything but liberating. He who came "to proclaim release to the
captives" told his followers to take upon themselves a yoke. He who was "to set at liberty them
that are bruised" bade those who were to be his
disciples to bear a cross. Although he liberated
men from legalistic literalism, he laid down principles which seem even more restrictive than the
old laws which he replaced. To restrain the lustful look and the angry feeling is certainly a more
strict limitation than to withhold oneself from the
acts of adultery or murder. In comparison with
our broad, easy indulgences, "Narrow is the gate,
and straitened the way, that leadeth unto life"
(Matthew 7. 14), as Jesus prescribed it for himself and his original disciples. And his Declaration of Independence, that "Whosoever would
save his life shall lose it, and whosoever shall
lose his life for my sake shall find it," seems in
direct contrast to the one enunciated by our
American founders that man has an inalienable
right "to life, liberty, and the pursuit of happiness."

The Christian Church has not succeeded very

well in resolving Jesus' paradoxical positions regarding freedom. Gilbert K. Chesterton, loyal to his Roman Catholic teaching, tries to refute the charge that the Church has taken the human cheerful Christ and made him inhuman and rigid. On the contrary, Chesterton declares the Church has made Jesus too mild and merciful.[1] It would be more accurate to say that the Church has been, and still is, guilty of misinterpreting Jesus in both directions. From Paul's day down to our own, there are those who translate Christian liberty into license and there are those who reduce Jesus' abundant life into a narrow and niggardly existence.

When we try to enter into Jesus' enigmatic secret of freedom, we come face to face with his narrow gate. The road to the Master's abundant spontaneous living is strait. In saying "Narrow is the gate, and straitened the way, that leadeth unto life," the Galilean Teacher was laying down the principle that discipline must precede genuine liberty. There seems nothing new or original about the mere statement of such a principle, for it has been reiterated by moral teachers from pre-Christian days down to the present time of Alexis Carrel. Yet about once in every generation it comes with a fresh force as the pendulum swings

---

[1] Gilbert K. Chesterton, *The Everlasting Man*, p. 212. Dodd, Mead and Company, New York.

from libertinism to Puritanism. Now that the
Freudian doctrine of self-expression has almost
exhausted its evangelistic fervor, we may be ready
for the Carrel prescription: "Two essential conditions for the progress of the individual are rela-
tive isolation and discipline. It is chiefly through
intellectual and moral discipline, and the rejec-
tion of the habits of the herd, that we can recon-
struct ourselves."[2] This is quite in line with
Jesus' injunction.

Life is an art. The interplay of our natures
with our environment is a complex process. A
person is free when he is able so to adjust himself
to his surroundings that he can obey and use the
laws of his own nature. Such freedom is not a
native gift, nor is it found, as Rousseau held, in
the state of nature. The free use of our full
nature is acquired as the musician wins the free
use of his instrument. The little girl must hold
herself to the patient finger exercises if she would
fit herself for that freedom of the artist whereby
her hands can dance up and down the keyboard
with unconscious grace while her mind follows the
theme of the composer. She might wish to forego
those finger exercises—and her neighbors might
wish even more that she would forego them—but
they have to be done. The artist's liberty comes
through discipline.

[2] Alexis Carrel, *Man, the Unknown*, p. 295. Harper and Brothers.

Freedom is not merely the sum of momentarily pleasant liberties any more than harmony is produced by striking all the keys of the piano at once or in succession. There must be co-ordination of impulses, timing of desires, rhythm of interests. The disciplines of Jesus do for our discordant desires what the leadership of a conductor does for a symphony orchestra.

This parallel between musical and spiritual culture was pursued recently by a talented New York woman in most interesting fashion. Through the channel of her rich musical knowledge, she was led to certain practices which make for artistry in religious expression.[3] Her experience is suggestive.

It is an inadequate, though not an inappropriate, analogy to say that Jesus played life as a Paderewski plays Mozart. He underwent his hours of rigorous personal discipline during the temptation in the wilderness. He maintained his periods of prayer which must have often been times of inward struggle, if we are to judge from the glimpse we get in Gethsemane. But what an artistic freedom he acquired for his public appearances! Involved problems and irritating interruptions never caused him to strike a false note or to lose the sureness of his touch. He had his own nature under such perfect control that he

[3] Anne Byrd Payson, *I Follow the Road.* The Abingdon Press.

never apparently had to struggle with any of our base physical temptations.

And what is more, he disciplined his desires into that state where he enjoyed doing his duty. The fourth Gospel may be giving quite a late afterthought in its report of Jesus at the well of Samaria, but nevertheless it gives a true reflection of his spirit in the reply which he made to his disciples on their return from dinner. When they urged him to eat, he is reported to have said, "My meat is to do the will of him that sent me, and to accomplish his work" (John 4. 34). He had reached the stage where duty is transformed into desire. That is the point to which the true artist attains. That is the point to which Christian discipline is designed to bring the art of living.

Life is a game as well as an art. Viewed in this aspect, it reveals the same need of the narrow gate. The foregoing of midnight suppers and club carousals is a necessary limitation which the football squad must undergo if its members would have freedom on the field. This is not the narrowness of asceticism, but of athleticism. It is in line with the training rules of the Nazarene coach. Jesus was not an ascetic about earthly enjoyments but he was in earnest about keeping them in their place.

Moreover, the zest of the game of life as well

as the freedom of it depends on discipline. That is the deeper truth which some of our disillusioned youth are now discovering. A recent spokesman of the school of self-expression and self-indulgence put it boldly when he confessed, "We took what we wanted, and now we find we no longer want what we took." The preservation of our very appetites and desires requires restriction. We can lock ourselves out of the full life by indulgence just as truly as we can lock ourselves in by narrowness.

It is the limitations of the game which help to give life to it. What would be the fun of baseball if each batter could strike at the ball as often as he pleased? It is the rule of "three strikes and out" that creates the interest.

Jesus showed a spirit of sportsmanship in passing through his own narrow gates. Aware of the meagerness of his materials, the shortness of his time, the obstacles placed by his enemies, and the immensity of his task, he exclaimed, "How am I straitened till it be accomplished!" (Luke 12. 50.) Yet he endured the limitations of circumstance as if they were the rules of the game rather than the restrictions of a prison. There was no bemoaning of his hardships, no beating against the bars of cruel fate. For a brief hour in Gethsemane, he prayed that the cup of sacrifice might pass from him. Yet he came forth to face the cross.

not with the broken spirit of a beaten contestant,
but after the manner of a gallant sportsman.

Jesus' secret of freedom at the circumference of
life lay in his discipline of the central impulses.
His principle was to control the entrances of the
mind and thereby prevent those complexes which
result from thwarting at the exits. Jesus started
his discipline with the eye, the imagination, the
thought. "Everyone that looketh on a woman to
lust after her hath committed adultery with her
already in his heart" (Matthew 5. 28). "Everyone who is angry with his brother shall be in danger of the judgment" (Matthew 5. 22). Such is
the inwardness of Jesus' moral commands.

The Galilean Teacher realized what our twen-
tieth-century psychologists are now telling us,
namely, that the imagination is ultimately more
powerful than the will. The selection of the pictures which are hung in the mind determines the
artistry of living. God has a pitiless publicity department. "There is nothing hid, save that it
should be manifested" (Mark 4. 22), is a principle
of the kingdom of God both in its individual and
social outworking. To restrain the angry thought
and the lustful look as Jesus did may seem to us
plainly restrictive, but it is far less emotionally de-
structive than to try to dam the passionate deeds
pouring out of a nature flooded with evil impulses.

Jesus' attitude toward discipline and freedom was somewhat like that of a certain contemporary uncle who had become the guardian of his orphaned nephew. The uncle took such pains in the nurturing of the lad's body and mind that when it came time for the latter to leave for college, the older man merely put his hands on his shoulders and said, "David, do what you have a mind to do." The youth had reached a stage of disciplined self-control where he could be trusted with his liberty. In like manner Jesus sought to build up the inner structure of character so that he could remove the outer scaffolding of rules and restrictions.

Jesus was not content merely to convert the will. He went on to cultivate the taste. He realized that a Christian's liberty depends on the Christlikeness of his tastes. That may seem a trite statement, but it is one which the Church has not seemed to grasp in its evangelism even down to rather recent days. The evangelistic emphasis has been to effect a redirection of will. The new convert was then left a raw recruit, so raw in fact that he could not maintain his own morale and all too often lapsed into what our fathers called the company of "backsliders," or what modern churchmen term "the inactive list." Religious education now seeks to remedy this defect by supplementary instruction. But thus far

Purpose of: To cultivate Christlike Tastes!

its results reach only a few, seldom many, beyond the teen age.

Jesus' inward discipline of thought and taste not only prevents those tensions which destroy the freedom and peace of action but also opens the way ahead for larger and freer use of life's essentials. By closing some of life's side doors we open the doors in front. By restricting some of the eye's sideshows we get a better view of the main objectives. Just as in the photographic studio the rear of the camera is covered with a cloth in order to get the focus, so Jesus, the Divine Photographer, counseled his followers that a narrowing of the vision is necessary to a clearing of the view. "The lamp of the body is the eye: if therefore thine eye be single, thy whole body shall be full of light" (Matthew 6. 22).

Selective seeing is a prerequisite to effective doing. Either Matthew in reporting or Jesus in speaking revealed a logical sequence when he followed the discussion of the "single eye" with the warning against the "serving of two masters." Like the witnesses of a magician's legerdemain, we frequently try to follow so many factors in a situation that we miss the essential point. And then, like Stephen Leacock's enthusiastic but futile knight who mounted his horse and rode off in all directions, our activity scatters itself in tributary ineffectiveness.

As the narrowing of the channel turns the shallow stream into a power-producing millrace, so the limitations of life often serve to generate force. When Beethoven was stricken with deafness he cried, "I will blunt the sword of fate," and with faculties thus narrowed, he forced his genius to create those incomparable compositions which release the listener into vast realms of beauty. When Helen Keller was left in infancy with the eye-gate, the ear-gate and the voice-gate closed, it seemed that she was destined to a meager fraction of life, but she inverted the fraction, making the denominator of her deficiencies into the numerator of her achievements, thus becoming one of the great figures of her generation. Jesus' earthly sphere was narrow, bounded laterally by a provincial nationalism and a sectarian ecclesiasticism, bounded terminally by a carpenter shop and a cross. But the very limitations of his circumstances heighten the distinction of his attainments.

And, finally, the implications of Jesus' principle of the narrow gate apply to the life hereafter as well as here. His intimations of immortality suggest not a state of being which we put on at death but a quality of being which we carry on through death. Jesus leads us to think that the entrance to eternal life is by way of earthly discipline rather than heavenly fiat. The Gospels picture Earth as a schoolroom which prepares us for heavenly living, rather than Heaven as a court-room which passes judgment on our earthly do-ing. The test is whether we have learned the life that can be independent of material things which moth and rust corrupt. If not, then we could have no heart in the spiritual life beyond the reach of such things, "for where thy treasure is, there will thy heart be also" (Matthew 6. 21). As for the person who has learned to like only the things of earth, no divine decree or judicial pardon can make him ready for heaven. Such a man would find no more freedom and enjoyment in a spir-itual heaven than a paroled convict with the habits and tastes of Sing Sing could find in a company of Christian mystics. The only persons to whom the hereafter can be heaven are those who have trained themselves to enjoy what Jesus enjoyed.

"Narrow is the gate, and straitened the way, that leadeth unto life"—eternal life—"and few be they that find it," for the many are still thinking of entrance by divine decree rather than divine discipline. They are concerned about getting by the Judge rather than about getting ready for the life beyond. The gate is narrow, due to the law of life and not the severity of the gatekeeper. Freedom here and hereafter requires discipline.

CHAPTER VIII

THE LIFTING YOKE

DURING much of the year the roads of Palestine have the look of a weary land. The relentless sun beating down and the grinding dust rolling up, the sleepy-eyed camels shuffling along as if about to drop, and their drivers trudging drearily beside them, women carrying bundles and waterpots on their heads, and bearded men looking old before their time— the whole scene is one of weariness.

This impression seems to have surged over Jesus as he journeyed from place to place, causing him one day to exclaim: "Come unto me, all ye that labor and are heavy laden, and I will give you rest. Take my yoke upon you, and learn of me; for I am meek and lowly in heart: and ye shall find rest unto your souls. For my yoke is easy, and my burden is light" (Matthew 11. 28-30).

Those words of Jesus are so familiar that we often fail to realize how remarkable they were, especially coming at the time indicated by the context as given in Matthew. For the first Gospel places this utterance in the midst of one of Jesus' most trying periods. His friends were deserting him, John the Baptist was doubting him, his

neighboring Galilean communities were turning
against him, his enterprise seemed collapsing
about him. Then just as the difficulties would
seem to have piled up to the backbreaking point,
the Master turns and says: "My yoke is easy, and
my burden is light."

It might almost be thought at first that such a
statement was spoken in irony, as if he were trying to rebuke those around him who were bemoaning their burdens. It might seem that Jesus
were saying: "You who think that you are heavy
laden, come and see a load that is a load. Take
my yoke upon you and see how light my burden
is." But no. Jesus was not speaking in irony,
nor was he pleading for pity. He was stating one
of his great paradoxical promises, namely, that he
can rest men with a yoke.

We are so accustomed to seeing Jesus portrayed
on the cross or in the agony of suffering that the
major emotion of many toward him is one of pity
or sympathy. We forget that when he walked in
the flesh he was the one to whom others came for
comfort and encouragement. There was something so youthfully vital about the Nazarene
Teacher that little children ran to play with him,
something so socially winsome that people wanted
him at their weddings, something so assuringly
strong that mourners and Magdalenes, poor
widows and worried young men of wealth came

to him for strength.   Burdened as he was with a superhuman task against overwhelming odds, he bore it with an abounding vitality which caused the weary and heavy laden to seek his secret.   He was the strange Man of the easy yoke.

Let us look into this paradox of the rest-giving yoke.

The first reason to appear is that it fits man's deepest needs.   Human nature is made for yoking.   Man belongs to the animal kingdom, but he is not meant to run wild.   He often thinks he is. He often feels that he would be so much happier if he could unharness himself from his loads of personal and social responsibilities and get "back to nature."   The cares of home, the routines of his job, the conventional restrictions of his community—all these pall on him at times, and he is tempted to cut loose, in some such fashion as Sinclair Lewis depicted in his *Babbitt* a few years ago.   We write books and scenarios about the call of the wild, that lure of the jungle which beckons us from the burdensome formalities and frictions of life.

But while there is a call of the wild, there is also a call of the yoke.   Down deep in human nature is something which makes even the gangster respond to the responsibility of caring for a crippled sister or a widowed mother; something which causes the carefree irresponsible wanderer to long for the burdens of "home, sweet home"; something which drives the prodigal son in the wild freedom of the far country to remember that even the servants in his father's house have comforts which he is missing; something which makes the retired business man restless, as he says, to be back in the harness, so that he may "wear out rather than rust out"; something which causes grandparents comfortably ensconced in their quiet corners to look back longingly to the long hours and heavy burdens of their early parenthood, realizing why a novelist once defined heaven as the place where all the parents are young and all the children are little.

Yes, human nature is designed for yoking. A man is not quite a man unless he is pulling more than his own weight. The altruistic impulses are as deeply rooted in him as are the selfish desires. One of the most fundamental needs of man's nature is the need to be needed.

Yonder is a man who has been self-analyzed and psychoanalyzed. He has learned what food is good for his digestion, what exercise is good for his body, what climate is good for his health. In fact, he has discovered about everything that is good for him, but withal he never seems to have found out what he is good for. Until he discovers that, he is restless and unhappy. And that is something which is not revealed by introspection or introversion. Man makes that discovery when he is called out of himself by some great cause or activity or need.

We appraise the value of our faculties as of our properties when they are taxed. When some challenge summons us to meet it, we learn new extensions of our strength and after expending ourselves in a crisis, we look back and say, "I did not know it was in me to do that much." When some neighbor in need comes to us in the midnight of his soul and we rise to give him, then we discover whether our spiritual larder contains the bread of life (compare Luke 11. 5-8).

We find out the cogency of our creeds when others bring us their doubts to be cleared. We awaken to the worth of our prayers when a loved one looks at us with great round eyes of pain and asks us to pray for him.

Until we feel the pull of being needed, we do not find rest unto our souls. Of course there are times when our weary bodies must be refreshed by relaxation. The Great Physician was well aware of this, and frequently said to his followers, "Come ye apart and rest awhile." But we soon get restless out of harness. Hence the Son of man, who came not to be ministered unto but to minister, knew that the souls of men could be ultimately happy only if they were ministering rather than being ministered unto. Therefore he said,

"Take my yoke upon you, . . . and ye shall find rest unto your souls."

Furthermore, Jesus made his yoke fit man's nature by adjusting it to individuals. It is quite possible that Jesus was drawing his figure of speech from the carpenter shop as well as from the traditional Hebrew expression, the "yoke of the law." As a carpenter, Jesus may have been a maker of yokes. If so, he knew that they had to be fitted to the contours of the animals which were to wear them. At any rate, Jesus individualized his requirements to fit cases. Or, rather, it is more accurate to say that the Great Physician did not deal with men as cases nor give factory-made rules in wholesale lots. Unlike present-day reformers and sociologists, he did not talk of masses or classes, or society or humanity. Jesus dealt with a man born blind, a centurion's servant, a publican named Zacchaeus, a certain man who had two sons. The Galilean Teacher did in the first century what a leading educator said our modern schools are now trying to do, namely, to deal with individuals although they come in groups.

And working with individuals rather than masses, he applied principles rather than rules. As we have said, Jesus distinguished between the ordinary personalities of the "Father level" and the gifted few of the "Kingdom level." Hence he did not tell Zacchaeus to do exactly that which he had commanded the rich young man. The former gave away half his goods, the latter was bidden to give away all. In trying to root out the cancerous growth of covetousness, some required a major operation, others a minor. Not all his followers were to forego marriage but only those "to whom it is given" (Matthew 19. 11). Jesus' primary concern was to keep the spirit of a man from breaking rather than to keep a rule from being broken.

When the meticulous ecclesiastical rule-makers of his day rebuked Jesus for healing on the Sabbath, he replied, "The sabbath was made for man, and not man for the sabbath" (Mark 2. 27). The scribes were concerned to preserve the institution of the sabbath; Jesus, to preserve the constitution of man. This focus of interest gave a flexibility to his yoke. Jesus increased the load of human responsibilities by widening the interests and sensitizing the sympathies; but he lessened the rigidity of method in carrying them. His yoke was a response to responsibilities rather than a restraint by rules. That made it easier.

A second revealing principle appears in this paradox of the easy yoke. Not only does it fit man's nature but it also steadies him. In the breaking of young animals to harness it is customary to team the fractious youngster with a tried and trusted elder. The steady teammate helps the fretful and chafing novice to learn its paces and keep its course.

So is it in the training of human beings. A wise mother does not merely say to the child, "Follow me." She yokes herself with the little one so that the child learns by trying to keep step with the grown-up, thereby acquiring both the direction and the tempo of the doing. Thus a good home is a partnership in which the experienced elders are teamed with the experimenting youngsters. Similarly, education is now using the project method, whereby teacher and student are teamed together in a partnership of free minds, fellow seekers after truth. Our universities do have some research men who display their achievements before pupils somewhat as a model in the store displays a dress before prospective customers; but the patient teacher plodding along beside the student is still indispensable to education. To make a true educational center, there is still needed a Mark Hopkins on the other end of a log, or, rather, on the other end of a yoke.

Likewise, the Master Teacher, the great Elder Brother, observed those who were wearing their nerves ragged, chafing at their restraints, sometimes plunging ahead too fast, sometimes lagging back dispiritedly or stubbornly, and he said, "Take my yoke upon you, and learn of me; for I am meek and lowly in heart." Jesus' meekness was not the broken spirit of a drudge horse but the patient steadiness of one who knows the laws and limitations of life and has learned to abide by them. Meekness, as Jesus used it here, is the attitude of one who submits himself to the laws of life as the scientist submits to the physical laws of nature, not trying to break them but to obey them and thus use them.

Repeatedly Jesus sought to develop in his disciples a patient adjustment to the divine time schedules. He reminded them that the kingdom of God is as a man casting into the ground seed which grows even while the man is sleeping, for "the earth beareth forth fruit of herself; first the blade, then the ear, then the full corn in the ear" (Mark 4. 28). The followers of Jesus were to gear their minds to the slow orderly processes of the soil rather than to the quick returns of the market place. And when they grew fretful at the delays of the Kingdom and the progress of its enemies, he told them the parable of the tares sowed by the enemies of a husbandman. When the farmer's servants saw the tares, they were eager to rush in and root them out, but he held them back saying, "Nay; lest haply while ye gather up the tares, ye root up the wheat with them. Let both grow together until the harvest" (Matthew 13. 29, 30).

To Jesus the judgments of God are sure, but he would not have his disciples expect to see the books balanced every week end. Nor would he have men by their shortsightedness and impatience destroy their own peace of mind and the progress of the Kingdom. "Which of you by being anxious can add one cubit unto his stature?" (Matthew 6. 27.) We cannot speed up our growth, and we should not borrow tomorrow's trouble in advance. "Sufficient unto the day is the evil thereof" (Matthew 6. 34).

It was this patient synchronization with the divine pace which gave Jesus his serenity under stress. When he stood before Pilate with the crowd clamoring for his blood and the governor prodding him with questions, his poise was unshaken. "Art thou the King of the Jews?" asked his inquisitor. "Thou sayest," calmly replied Jesus. The fourth Gospel adds a sentence which makes vocal the secret of such composure: "Every one that is of the truth heareth my voice" (John 18. 37). He felt no need to enter into heated defense. He was never stampeded into feverish or blustering argument. Believing that truth was on his side, he could trust his cause to time.

The yoke of Jesus was easy because it teamed the wearer with One of unflustered temper and unhurried tempo, with One who took his stride with the centuries rather than with the hours,

One who did not chafe at delays and reverses because he was confident of eventual victory.

And finally, a third reason may be suggested to explain the paradox of the easy yoke. It sustains the wearer as well as fits and steadies him.

Saint Augustine, in one of his sermons, likens the yoke of Jesus to the plumage of a bird—an easy weight which enables it to soar into the sky. It is another of the seeming contradictions of life that weights do often help us to rise. What husband is there who has not more than once been kept up in the hour of temptation or adversity by the thought of the wife who relies on him and has trusted her life to his support? What father is there who has not often been helped to rise with unexpected energy by remembering the family whose responsibility rests on him?

Recently a Princeton alumnus was telling of his college experience. He had come to the beginning of his senior year with a record none too good. In fact, it was somewhat problematical whether he would be graduated because of his irregularities and dare-deviltry. One day Woodrow Wilson, then president of Princeton, called him in and told him that the faculty had appointed him to a position of responsibility on the campus. That weight of responsibility saved the student's career. Rising in response to it, he finished his course with credit.

This was a principle which Jesus used in straightening men up. He took the shifting, unsteady Simon and said, "Thou art Peter, and upon this rock I will build my church" (Matthew 16. 18). And Peter rose to the responsibility, becoming the prime pillar of early Christendom.

But the lifting power of Jesus' yoke involves something more than the stimulus it gives to the wearer's own exertion. It calls into play one of life's deepest laws, namely, that the biggest and best things yield their highest uses to those who are willing to be used by them. Some forces in life give themselves only to those who surrender to them. This, of course, is not true of everything. A motor car, for example, is a man's tool for travel. He does not have to surrender himself to his car in order to get its benefits. So is it with a man's relation to the bank which handles his money or to the press which brings him his news. These are merely instruments of living to be used by him.

But when we turn from cars and banks to the realm of music or love or religion, it is different. A person can get some benefits from music merely by trying to use it for his recreation or relaxation. But the satisfactions derived by a person just playing for his own amusement are small compared with those felt by an Iturbi when he is giving himself to music to be used for the interpretation of a great theme. The great artist is not seeking mere self-expression, he is trying to express something through himself. Thereby he gives and gets the greatest joy. By surrendering himself to his art he feels the lift and power of it.

Likewise is it with love. We can use a home and thereby make it yield us some very substantial benefits, such as shelter, comfort, security. But these are meager in comparison with the solid joys of a home wherein the members are motivated by devotion to others. Love gives its highest values only to those who give themselves to it.

Jesus was applying this same principle when he said that his yoke was easy and his burden was light. Those who surrender to him receive a reciprocating surrender of his power to them, just as the artist is carried away by his inspiration and the lover is lifted by his love. The service of his kingdom is not a burden but a support.

In saying this we have to convey the added thought of Jesus as the continuing comrade in his yoke. When he offered his yoke, it was for union with himself as coworker. There is something more personal about this relationship than about that between an artist and his art or a devotee and his work. Jesus imparted a feeling of himself as the Eternal Contemporary. If the last words of Matthew be regarded as an interpolation, it should be remembered that they were

added by followers who felt the truth and power
of Jesus' promise: "Lo, I am with you alway,
even unto the end of the world" (Matthew 28.
20).

That sense of personal comradeship and co-
operation makes for the uniqueness of Jesus
among the founders of religion. He did something more than to set the moral standard to be
reached, more even than to set the pace of advance
toward it. He was like the Alpine guide who
goes ahead but ropes himself to those who follow.
What mountain climber struggling and stagger-
ing on the steep cliff complains about the weight
of the rope which links him to his leader? That
rope is a yoke which lifts.

CHAPTER IX

THE MEEK MASTER

THERE was an air of mastery about Jesus.
"They were astonished at his teaching: for
he taught them as having authority, and not
as the scribes" (Mark 1. 22). It was more than
the mastery of a teacher who knew his subject.
Jesus' authoritative manner extended over personalities as well as over fields of study. "They
were all amazed, insomuch that they questioned
among themselves, saying, What is this? a new
teaching! with authority he commandeth even
the unclean spirits, and they obey him" (Mark 1.
27). There was the kind of authority about the
Carpenter from Nazareth which caused a Roman
centurion, who was accustomed to give orders and
have them obeyed, to feel that Jesus possessed a
similar power whereby he could command and
exact obedience. "Say the word, and my servant
shall be healed" (Luke 7. 7).

From the day when his neighbors set upon him
after his initial speech at Nazareth to the hour
when he stood before Pilate with the crowd outside clamoring for his blood, Jesus was master of
every situation which the Gospels portray. No
sudden surprises ever shook his poise. No shat-

THE MEEK MASTER   109

tering disasters left him dumbfounded. He never
appeared driven or frightened or harried.

When he was acclaimed by the crowd as king,
he did not lose his head. When he was cursed by
the crowd as an impostor, he did not lose his
nerve. Fawned upon by the flattering Pharisees
at their dinners, he did not soften his sayings.
Spat upon by the mob, he did not harden his
heart. In public and in private, in joy and in
sorrow, on the Mount of Transfiguration and in
the Garden of Gethsemane, he was the one to
whom others instinctively turned for orders and
for order.

The fourth Gospel is true to the spirit of the
Synoptists when it pictures Jesus with a towel and
basin asserting: "Ye call me Teacher, and Lord:
and ye say well; for so I am" (John 13. 13).
There was something lordly even in the stoop of
Jesus.

Paradoxical is it, therefore, when this masterful
One says: "I am meek and lowly in heart" (Matthew 11. 29). Meekness seems at the other end
of the scale from masterfulness. To be sure, even
dictators have their moods of humility. Proud
kings at times are conscience-stricken and confess
their sins and weakness. But as we have seen,
Jesus never appears to have had that haunting
and humbling sense of sin which clouds the sum-
mits of sainthood and greatness. His assertion of

meekness was not a confession but a promise. It
was not spoken during a momentary ebbing of
Jesus' flooding energy. It was no mere revelation of a mood.

Jesus was deliberately declaring his possession
of a quality which men were to learn of him.
They were to learn it because it made for mastery and achievement. "Blessed are the meek:
for they shall inherit the earth" (Matthew 5. 5).
Moods of humility in the midst of victory would
be quite understandable; but meekness as a means
to mastery—that is the paradox.

Jesus' use of the word "meek" serves to clear
away some of the popular misconceptions which
have clustered about the term. To many the
word suggests a servile manner, the outward expression of an inferiority complex. Clearly there
was nothing of that in the masterful Jesus, and
noteworthy is it that Matthew introduces the
declaration of meekness with one of Jesus' most
sweeping assertions of authority: "All things have
been delivered unto me of my Father: and no
one knoweth the Son, save the Father" (Matthew
11. 27).

Nor could Jesus have meant by meekness a
shrinking shyness. The common expression,
"meek as a mouse," suggests those persons who in
their desire for self-effacement slip around the
corners of rooms and yet seem always to be getting

under the feet of others—human beings about as unattractive as the little animals to which they are likened. It is one thing to lose your life in something larger; it is another to keep erasing yourself from pictures with smudging self-consciousness. The former attitude is advocated by Him who said, "Whosoever shall lose his life for my sake shall find it;" the latter misconception of meekness is explicitly contrary to the command: "Let your light shine before men, that they may see your good works, and glorify your Father which is in heaven" (Matthew 5. 16).

No, the meek man, as Jesus suggests him, is not the shrinking fellow who seeks the corners, nor is he the spiritless person who appears cowed when cornered. When they see themselves caught, our modern gunmen are often reported as submitting meekly to arrest. Such is but the cowardly gesture of helplessness in defeat. Jesus, on his part, never acknowledged defeat, and there is one word which even the bitterest and most malignant persecutors of Jesus never applied to him. It was the word "coward."

The reports of Jesus' arrest and trial convey the impression not of a prisoner beaten into supine submission but of a person who held his peace because of an inner sense of power and victory untouched by the turbulence of the time. Christlike meekness is not an attitude born of defeat but a quality productive of victory. "Blessed are the meek: for they shall inherit the earth."

Having suggested what Jesus did *not* mean by meekness, let us look into what he *did* mean. Gentleness is perhaps the best single synonym, yet that should be simplified. The Hebrew derivation connotes a disposition of the heart susceptible of being molded by the spirit of God in contrast with an attitude of defiant self-will. Matthew has set Jesus' claim to meekness in a context which bears out the Hebrew connotation. It is from a prayer of communion stressing the submission of Son to Father, that Jesus turns to offer his restful yoke to the weary and assert his own meekness of heart.

The meek man is the God-molded man, the divinely tempered spirit. Just as the smithy tempers the iron into steel, so Jesus' nature was tempered in the fire of the wilderness temptation, and on the anvil of Gethsemane. Similarly, this is what seemed to take place in the character of Moses, the only other biblical figure to whom the word "meek" is explicitly applied. The young scion of Pharaoh's house, becoming impatient at the ingratitude and perversity of the Israelites whom he was trying to save, lost his temper. God had then to "temper" him into meekness. And as the heat and hammering transform the porous brittleness of the crude iron into the firm flexibility of steel, so the God-tempering process makes the meek man firmer and yet more flexible. That is in part the paradox of meekness.

In this sense the physical scientist is meek when he confronts natural laws. He does not rebel against them in futile protest, nor does he resign himself to them in helpless submission. He does not fight nature; he uses nature. If his experiments fail, the failures do not break his faith in the scientific principle. He varies his method. Long experience in the laboratory tempers the brash cocksureness of the beginner into the firmer faith in the scientific principle and into more flexibility as to claims and methods of application.

This blending of firmness with flexibility was manifest in Jesus' mastery of life's inevitables. The supreme revelation of his resourcefulness was not in his astute handling of crowds, his clever confounding of critics, his mysterious control over material things. Greater than his ability to handle the movable elements of his environment was his superb control in those situations wherein things could not be moved and he had to stand and take it, "and having done all, to stand."

Jesus was averse to that supine and superficial resignation which accepts needless suffering and limitations as the "will of God." We cannot think of Jesus standing by the bier of a child dead through neglect or malnutrition, and piously saying: "Be not rebellious in spirit. God took him." Nor can we picture the Master standing amid the slain bodies on a battlefield and exhorting the survivors, explaining, "This is God's will." Jesus was not among those who mildly submit to the damnable stupidities of men as if they were sent by his Heavenly Father. Like Robert Louis Stevenson, he would not have the "false winter-green plant" of such pious resignation in the garden of his mind. Jesus would have his followers summon all their resources to ward off accident, disease, and death. When he sent out his disciples on their exploratory expedition early in his ministry, he bade them be "wise as serpents and harmless as doves," in avoiding needless opposition and persecution. But when man has done his best, there is bound to be a residuum of inevitable suffering and frustration to which he must submit.

And Jesus, with all his advocacy of wisdom to prevent needless pain, nevertheless stood up to it when it came. He prayed that the cup might pass from him, but when he saw it was inevitable, he drank it. "Father, if thou be willing, remove this cup from me: nevertheless not my will, but thine, be done" (Luke 22. 42). He drank it with the smile of a winning sportsman—"Be of good cheer; I have overcome the world" (John 16. 33). He drank it without becoming bitter toward his

fellow men who helped to inflict it—"Father, forgive them; for they know not what they do"
(Luke 23. 34). He drank it without losing faith
in the goodness of the God who allowed the pain
to come—"Father, into thy hands I commend my
spirit" (Luke 23. 46). In all this we see meekness, the God-tempered quality which keeps a
spirit flexible yet firm in the face of frustration
that would break down the brittle defiance of
self-will.

Christlike meekness includes also the element
of patience. Jesus took his stride from the centuries rather than the seconds. Jesus could afford
to wait for vindication because he knew time was
on his side. When he stood before Pilate, he was
not like a man fighting desperately with his back
to the wall; he was a man standing confidently
with his face to the future. He did not defend
himself; he waited calmly for time and truth to
testify for him. "To this end have I been born,
and to this end am I come into the world, that I
should bear witness unto the truth. Everyone
that is of the truth heareth my voice" (John 18.
37, 38). Jesus stood in the presence of the powerful Pilate as Maxwell Anderson in his drama
makes Mary of Scotland stand before the im-
prisoning Elizabeth, and say, "Nevertheless, I
win." Such meekness of bearing is not the cring-
ing of a caught criminal but the quietness of a

conqueror confident that his victory is inevitable though delayed.

The person who learns the meekness of Jesus does not chafe at the bit of restraint nor fret himself at life's inevitable delays. Neither does he have to prance and bluster to display his strength. He possesses such a sure sense of power that he does not need to be noisy and assertive in showing it. There is such a thing as being too strong to fight as well as "too proud to fight."

Along with this patient strength and flexible firmness of Christian meekness goes the quality of modesty. Jesus himself manifested no humbling sense of his own imperfection, but he did reveal a consciousness of his own insufficiency apart from his Heavenly Father. His followers have both to keep them modest. It is the deflating sense of imperfection and insufficiency which makes us "poor in spirit" so that we can "be filled" with the Spirit of God. The man who thinks he has arrived is the one who never gets going. The meek man is he who knows how far short of perfection he is and therefore keeps growing.

This modesty of meekness, however, is due not merely to a consciousness of imperfection but also to self-forgetfulness. The meek man is not always standing on his rights and looking for his share of credit. Consequently, he is insensitive to personal insults and indifferent to acclaim. A popu-

lar columnist some years ago reflected this in a
definition of humility. "It is the wish to be great
and the dread of being called great. It is the wish
to help and the dread of thanks. It is the love of
service and the distaste for rule. It is trying to
be good and blushing when caught at it" (Dr.
Frank Crane). Such a definition of humility is
not far from the kingdom-of-God conception of
modesty as an element of meekness.

Having thus analyzed Jesus' formula of meekness, let us ask whether such a formula does work
to "inherit the earth." We have already suggested
part of the answer. The meek man's tempered
flexibility of firmness is not only effective in mastering the inevitables, but it is a most forceful
quality in winning a way through everyday situations. In a certain home is a patient wife married
to a husband of the blustering type. He wants
what he wants when he wants it. He thunders in
argument and storms at every frustration. The
mild and gentle wife often yields the point, but
in the long run she almost invariably gets her way.
She loses the battle but wins the campaign. The
meek spirit sees the wisdom of yielding the immediate and the secondary for the sake of securing the main objective. Furthermore, when
meekness has to cut through opposition, it does
so with a fineness of edge due to its divine temper-
ing. Abraham Lincoln felt constrained finally

to use force in order to save the life of the Union, but tempered into meekness, as he was, he cut with a kindly sharpness which made for a speedy healing of the wounds.

The modesty of the meek is also a factor which makes for success, even as the world measures that word. There is a very apparent practical wisdom in the words of Jesus, "Whosoever shall exalt himself shall be humbled; and whosoever shall humble himself shall be exalted" (Matthew 23. 12). Pride goeth before a fall because the proud man tends to trip himself up—and others seem glad to assist him in doing it. The twelve-year-old boy was unwittingly putting his finger on this truth when he pointed to the picture of Charles I on the way to the scaffold and explained to his little brother, "That is King Charles on his way to being blockheaded." Pride stops growth and stiffens opposition. Modesty keeps a person studying and enlists the co-operation and comradeship of others. The humble publican goes into the kingdom of heaven before the proud Pharisee.

Furthermore, the meek man saves for other uses so much energy which the proud person wastes on keeping his standing, warding off slights, and fretting over those who get ahead.

Moreover, the meek inherit the earth after the others lose it. The aggressive fighters may gain a temporary rule and spread their domains with mushroomlike growth, but they fail in managing the power after they get it. The medieval kings blustered and battled their way over Europe, dividing the spoils of the fallen Roman Empire; but they exhausted themselves in internecine strife and allowed their power to slip into the hands of the monasteries. The meek monk with his cowl came into possession of what the king with his crown had forfeited. In modern Europe, to be sure, the Church has lost that power back to the State, but is it not also true that in countries like Spain, France, Russia, and Mexico, the Church that has lost its prestige is the Church which has lost its meekness? Dictators, whether in State or Church, sooner or later set themselves above law, and their powers pass to those meeker spirits who have learned how to master life by submitting to its laws.

One of the tragic failures of traditional Christianity is that it has inculcated the personal virtues which have helped men to secure power but has not preserved in those men the qualities which insure the right use of power. The drunkards have been made sober. The shiftless have been turned to thrift. Slaves of passion have been given self-control; and those virtues of sobriety, thrift, self-control, and their like, have lifted man to positions of mastery and power. Then, too, often they lost their meekness. They began to misuse their power for selfish, unsocial, or sordid purposes. And misused power is short-lived.

Furthermore, the principle of mastery of natural law by scientific meekness, has its parallel in the sphere of personality. As scientists master laws by serving them, so we master men by serving them. Jesus said: "The rulers of the Gentiles lord it over them, and their great ones exercise authority over them. Not so shall it be among you: but whosoever would become great among you shall be your minister; and whosoever would be first among you shall be your servant" (Matthew 20. 25-27). In saying that, Jesus was not merely setting up a new system of grading greatness; he was reversing the methods of prevailing social organization. Ordinarily, movements like that which Jesus was inaugurating started by enlisting the rich and ruling classes. Since the aim was to spread them by influence, it would seem logical to lead off with influential people. Jesus did not proceed on that principle. He began with the poor, plain people. So significant was this that Professor John Macmurray holds, "It is this discovery of the common people that is Jesus' great contribution to social history."[1]

But in his statement regarding servants and masters, was Jesus not doing something more

---

[1] *Creative Society*, p. 44. Eddy and Page.

than reversing the rank and changing the method of organization? Was he not reminding his followers of the frequently forgotten law that the servants eventually prove to be the real rulers of their masters? The Gentile principle of mastery by conquest makes the subject dependent but eager to be independent. The Christian rule of mastery by service makes the servant so indispensable that the other does not desire to be independent of him. Signor Marconi, for example has made Italy more securely his subject by putting his electrical genius at the service of his people than will Signor Mussolini by his dominating policy of overlordship. And even though Italy has subdued Ethiopia by military conquest, it will be a Pyrrhic victory compared to the possible mastery which might have been hers by serving the little sister nation. The Son of man has spread his rule by the principle of ministering service. He makes himself indispensable to those who allow him to serve them. Those who have used his service feel that they cannot get along without him. They remain dependent on him. Mastery through service is not a mere ideal for a future kingdom: it is a principle that works in this world. The serving Pasteurs retain the hearts of a people when the Napoleons have gone into the discard. The meek do inherit the mastery of the earth.

And while they are achieving this control through service, the meek enjoy the values of the earth, regardless of the legal ownership. "A man's life consisteth not in the abundance of the things which he possesseth" (Luke 12. 15). There is a power of appropriating values to which others hold the title. The meek have the secret of such appropriation. Who owns the masterpiece matters not to the meek. They revel in its beauty. The collecting of rare editions is the privilege of those who have the money. But the enjoyment of them is the privilege of those who can appreciate their intrinsic worth.

Dickens, in *David Copperfield,* pictures Traddles as poor as a church mouse, yet merry as a grig with his young wife trudging gleefully by his side gloating over the gorgeous display of London's most famous stores. They never expected to own these costly articles, but they could do without them, and rejoice in each other more because they did not covet them. Also the great noncompetitive treasures of earth and sky—glorious sunsets, mountain vistas, luxuriant foliage—these are the possession of the meek. In fact, life's ultimate values—beauty, truth, and goodness—are all noncompetitive. And these are the inheritance of the meek.

The Gentile principle of overlordship gives power *over;* the Christian principle of service

gives power *for*.   There is some satisfaction in
mastering a motor car or a business organization.
But it is meager compared to the satisfaction of
being mastered by a great cause or a great love.
And posterity remembers men by the causes which
they served rather than by the number of subjects
or soldiers who served them.   The leaders of
armies may win the day's acclaim; but the servants
of causes are chosen for the Halls of Fame.
Doubly blessed are the meek, for they both enjoy
and possess.

CHAPTER X

THE INDEPENDENT CO-OPERATOR

THE key principle of Jesus' ethics was reverence for personality. By this he tested laws, institutions, customs. His sensitive regard for the individual was based on his sense of each person's divine worth. Every man was a child of God. The very hairs of his head were numbered. Everything that happened to a human being was of concern to his Heavenly Father who keeps track of falling sparrows and regards man as of more value than many sparrows.

The individual was not to be lost sight of in this world or in the next. When the Sadducees interviewed him about the resurrected life, Jesus reminded them that God had said, "I am the God of Abraham, and the God of Isaac, and the God of Jacob." Then he added, "God is not the God of the dead, but of the living" (Matthew 22. 32). That statement, made long after the patriarchs were dead, implies Jesus' belief in the persistence of individual personality.

Since each person was of such value in the eyes of God, the society of men must be organized to safeguard his individuality. The sparkling spontaneity of childhood must not be stifled.

The ties of family, even his own, must not hold a
man back from following his call of duty.   The
laws of State must not commandeer the conscience
but leave each free "to render . . . unto Caesar
the things which are Caesar's; and unto God the
things that are God's" (Matthew 22. 21).   The
Pharisees had allowed the rigid routines of traditional religious observances to make them like
"whited sepulchers," but Jesus went about his
kingdom's work with the fresh exuberance of a
bridegroom coming from his chamber.

If individuality was to be preserved, certain
corollaries followed.   Independence of judgment
was not only a right but an obligation.   Jesus set
the example by asserting his own right to think
and speak for himself in contradistinction to the
lawmakers "of old time."   He scathingly rebuked
the Pharisees who made the traditional prayers in
public to be seen of men.   He required his disciples to think through their own convictions.
When he asked them what men were saying as to
his own identity and they gave him the current
reports, that did not satisfy Jesus.   He countered
with another query: "But whom say ye that I
am?"   Then came Peter's great assertion, "Thou
art the Christ."   Whereupon Jesus made a significant reply: "Blessed art thou, Simon Bar-
Jonah: for flesh and blood hath not revealed it
unto thee, but my Father which is in heaven"

(Matthew 16. 17). In other words, the value of Simon's belief was that he had not merely taken the word of some other person but had worked out his own first-hand conviction.

Along with this essential individuality of judgment was to go personal initiative. Those who would enter into the kingdom of heaven must manifest a righteousness which exceeds the righteousness of the scribes and Pharisees. They were expected to go "the second mile" and to turn "the other cheek." Crowd morality was not enough. Jesus demanded something more dynamic than mere decency, something more redemptive than mere respectability.

The preparation for the Kingdom is somewhat similar to the building of a road. First, the seers and prophets go ahead to chart the line of future travel. They at personal risk take advanced positions in their generation which their posterity will take for granted. After the seers come the blasters, those daring nonconformists who shock their contemporaries and blow up obstructing prejudices. Then follow God's "construction gang" to lay the road which the masses can travel. Jesus made clear that progress follows those pioneering, adventurous spirits who keep bursting out ahead, the social rebels who revolt against established economic and political injustices.

The preservation of personal initiative is necessary, not only to insure social progress but also to maintain individual interest. With his unmatched knowledge of human nature, Jesus knew that group action must be interlarded with individual effort in order to keep up the morale. Rather early in his ministry he sent out his followers on a mission of teaching and healing through the countryside. That deputation of disciples going out, two by two, was like the sending of a lecture class into the laboratory for practice work. It is the individual experimentation which clarifies and vivifies instruction. In the study of medicine the long, severe regime frequently causes students to drop out of the course from loss of interest and lack of effort, but when at last the young interne is given some patients to practice on in the hospital, some of the patients may drop out of the course but the embryo doctor stays on, for he has learned the thrill of the first-hand practice of medicine. The Great Physician realized how essential to sustained zeal is personal initiative.

Moreover, his regard for the individual carried with it the call for personal responsibility. The rights of independence and initiative are safeguarded only by the assumption of responsibility. Each man is accountable for his actions. While Jesus recognized that calamities and afflictions come upon individuals often through no fault of their own, he gave no justification to those who would offer external circumstances as the complete alibis for their misdeeds. In the current of forces which play upon our lives, there is some point at which a man is responsible for the direction of the channel. When he saw men searching for signs of divine intervention and shifting responsibility to external powers, he rebuked them, saying, "Why even of yourselves judge ye not what is right?" (Luke 12. 57.)

The fourth Gospel caught the true echo, if not the actual voice, of Jesus in the closing conversation with Peter which it reports. Peter is pictured as looking around at John and asking what the latter is to do. Jesus replied, "If I will that he tarry till I come, what is that to thee? follow thou me" (John 21. 22). The call of duty comes like the path of light from the rising sun across a lake directly to the foot of the observer. One of the points at which Jesus pioneered beyond his predecessors was that he made the individual rather than the group the governing factor in human relations.

But, on the other hand, no one ever stressed the necessity of interdependence more penetratingly than Jesus. Paul reflects Jesus' paradoxical blending of independence and interdependence in his letter to the Galatians: "Bear ye one another's burdens, and so fulfill the law of Christ;" and then three sentences later, "For each man shall bear his own burden" (Galatians 6. 2, 5). Jesus' principle of independence was more than that of tolerance, to "live and let live." It was, rather, that of co-operation, "to live and help live."

Jesus saw that individualism defeats itself. When everyone is guided only by his desire to get what he pleases, no one gets what he pleases. This truth is entering into the grain of our thought as living grows more complex. Dean Wicks of Princeton makes it vivid by a simple citation. Our grandfathers, he reminds us, went to school in little one-room country schoolhouses with windows and doors opening on the ground floor. If a fire broke out in such a building, it was quite enough to cry: "Fire! Everybody for himself!" But now our children study in large city school buildings, several stories high and housing often several hundred pupils. If a fire should break out in one of these modern structures and the cry were raised, "Everybody for himself," the result would be panic, disaster, probably death. The crowded complicated world of our day requires co-ordination for safety as well as freedom.

The preservation of vital culture calls for great individuals, but not for individualists. Another Princeton dean, Doctor Gauss, points out the distinction. "The individualist achieves his position only by virtue of what he subtracts from others;

by what he devotes exclusively to his own use. The individual, on the other hand, is great by what he bestows upon others through no loss to himself."[1] Jesus came to liberate the forces of individuality by checking the forces of individualism.

In doing so his primary method was by influence rather than by interference. To be sure, he did restrain the money-changers; he did talk once or twice about a sword; and he urged some sharp surgical restrictions, but the major symbols of his method were salt and leaven and light. "Ye are the salt of the earth. . . . Ye are the light of the world" (Matthew 5. 13, 14). "The kingdom of heaven is like unto leaven" (Matthew 13. 33). His attitude was somewhat similar to that of a new college president whose first matriculation address a few years ago evoked a hearty response from the student body. In the course of it this educator declared that he was opposed to a lot of rules which often clutter campus life. But, he said, there are certain conventions which gentlemen observe everywhere. Those conventions would be maintained in that college. What was it that made the students like the temper of that talk? The fact that he used the word "conventions" for the old-fashioned word "rules"? No. It was that he impressed his hearers as a gentle-

---

[1] Christian Gauss, *A Primer for Tomorrow*, p. 294. Charles Scribner's Sons.

man setting a style of conduct without much conscious effort to impose it upon them. It was an illustration of the influence of personality reaching minds steeled against preaching, propaganda, and reform.

So Jesus set a style of co-ordinated living rather than stressed regulations or legislation. He did not give the impression of a present-day propagandist bent on putting across a program. He relied more on the shadow of his influence than on the shouts of appeal. He took time to play with little children, to attend wedding suppers, to visit the mourning. His personality overshadowed his program. Does not this fact account for the further fact that his power cannot be adequately summed up in any specializing or professional words? Jesus was the world's premier Preacher, but we do not comprehend him by calling him a pulpiteer. He was a Teacher towering above all others in effectiveness, but it is not enough to call him a pedagogue or educator. Jesus worked such fundamental reforms that the world has not been the same since, but we certainly would not reflect the gospel portrait by calling him a reformer. No, there is only one word spacious enough to embody the unprofessionalized wholeness of his nature. He was the Man of Nazareth, setting a style of living for the sons of men.

Working primarily by influence rather than by interference, he pointed the way into the co-ordination of our independence with our interdependence. As has been said, Jesus had such sensitive reverence for personality that he would safeguard the individual's independence from the encroachments of the group. And, on the other hand, he taught with unparalleled insistence the necessity of controlling one's personal liberty from endangering our interdependence. Jesus was against individualism as well as against regimentation.

To avoid both these evils and to relieve the tensions created when the spirit of independence confronts the necessity of interdependence, Jesus would drive self-control and social control together, but in tandem fashion with the former ahead. He would have his followers realize that the individual secures his freedom from encroachments by restraining his liberty from encroaching on others. That is a point which the advocates of economic *laissez faire* fail to see on their side, and which the enthusiastic proponents of communistic Utopias overlook on their side.

Suppose a person were the owner of a plot of ground at the very center of Manhattan Island. Suppose that he were to say, "Inasmuch as the ground is mine, I shall proceed to build on it as high as I please." But the city says, "No, you will have to limit the height of your building, for

you must consider the shadow which your structure casts." "All right," replies the owner, "then
I shall make use of my property by digging down
until I strike gas and have my own fuel supply."
Again the city answers, "No, you cannot drill for
gas here in the center of New York for you must
have regard to the atmosphere you release." If
the plot were out on the open prairie, the owner
could go as high and as deeply as he desired, but
the value of the property would hardly make it
worth while. For what makes the value of that
corner at the heart of Manhattan? Mainly the
fact that so many people wish to live around it,
but also the fact that those who do dwell there
must have concern for the shadow which they cast
and the atmosphere which they release. It is by
such holding of property and personality that we
maintain the values of democracy and make a
Christian civilization.

Herein we see illustrated a self-control which
has its eye to social implications and a social control which has concern for individual liberty.
That is a combination which Jesus would foster.
He stood for a socialized self-control and also
for an individualized social control.

The former principle runs like a bedrock
beneath Jesus' precepts of individual morality.
It crops out in situations like that of the rich
young man who came to him for the secret of

eternal life. He had kept the Ten Commandments. But Jesus bade him go and sell his property and give the proceeds to the poor. In the
light of Jesus' other teachings regarding possessions, this command could hardly have meant that
the way to eternal life is to supplement the Ten
Commandments with communal ownership. No,
Jesus seems to have been testing the man's social-
ization of insight and motive. It is one thing to
care enough for oneself to refrain from doing
harm to others; it is quite another thing to care
enough for others to have a passion for doing
them good. It is the part of a gentleman to be
decent with a distaste for unrighteousness. It is
the mark of a Christian to "hunger and thirst
after righteousness." The young man had attained ethical self-control but he lacked the truly
social motive.

Jesus called for the practice of the Golden Rule,
but with far more insight than most persons use.
The trouble with too many of us in this matter
of doing unto others as we would that they should
do unto us is that we do not use imagination
enough to know what we would wish done to us
if we were in the other fellows' places. Consequently, we do what we think is good for them
and that usually irritates them. Dives is not
recorded as having any ill-will toward the beggar
who lay at his gate. He merely did not try to

enter into the poor man's situation. Those who stood condemned in Jesus' picture of the Last Judgment did so because they had not noticed. Jesus, on the other hand, so put himself into the shoes of others that he could say, "Inasmuch as ye did it unto one of these my brethren, even these least, ye did it unto me" (Matthew 25. 40).

Unless men do develop this socialized self-control, they will lose their liberties in repressive and burdensome social controls. Jesus pointed this out. It was a note of plain practical wisdom which he struck when he counseled: "Agree with thine adversary quickly, while thou art with him in the way; lest haply the adversary deliver thee to the judge, and the judge deliver thee to the officer, and thou be cast into prison" (Matthew 5. 25). Courts, prisons, costly legislation are the alternatives to individual self-control. And external social controls are never a satisfactory substitute for personal initiative and discipline. Two selfish individualists do not make a happy marriage, however strict the divorce laws by which they are held together. A thousand irresponsible inhabitants do not make a successful community, however perfect the social planning under which they are to live.

To say this, however, is not to endorse those conservatives of the *status quo* who declare that social systems cannot be improved until individuals are corrected. Souls and systems are so interrelated that they must be changed together. The abolition of gladiatorial combats in Rome and of Negro slavery in America did not wait for the conversion of a majority of the citizenry. "The kingdom of heaven is like unto leaven." It spreads and lifts with a wizardry of power. One thoroughly Christian individual in a home can change the atmosphere of a whole household. A dozen saintly souls in a church can set a spiritual pace for the entire parish. A few leaders in a community or state can leaven the public policy.

When Paul Robeson, the great Negro singer, played on the football squad at Rutgers College, it happened that a game was scheduled one season with a team from the South. When the Southern team arrived at Rutgers and learned that a Negro was to play against it, the captain at first served notice that his squad would not play under such conditions. Whereupon the Rutgers captain replied that *they* would either play with Robeson on the team or they would not play at all. The game, therefore, began in a spirit none too good. Things were made difficult for the Negro. But Robeson played without rancor. When the game was over, a deputation from the Southern team waited upon Robeson and apologized. What changed the temper of that team and the atmosphere of the game? Not the referee or the regulations, but the sportsmanlike playing of an individual.

Jesus planned his kingdom program with full knowledge that there was no social substitute for individual effort. But he also knew that the very interdependence of life enables the individual spirit to leaven whole groups.

Thus the Son of man came to save both souls and systems. The system which does not develop the individual is not a saving one. And the individual who is not working to leaven the system is not a saved one.

CHAPTER XI

THE UNSELFISH PROFIT MOTIVE

THE incentive of reward seems contrary to the general content of Jesus' teaching. Wages and profits belong not to the language of love, which was the Master's central motivating principle. The thought of prizes or pay does not keep company with the cross. The followers of Jesus were "to lend, hoping for nothing again"; they were to love enemies and not merely those who loved in return; they were to throw in their lot with a leader who was poorer than the foxes of the field in that he "had not where to lay his head." In illustrating Jesus' offer to his recruits one might paraphrase the famous challenge of Garibaldi: "Ahead of you lie homeless nights and foodless days, social scorn and physical persecution; for all of you the cross of sacrifice and for some of you the cross of death. You who love God and his kingdom, follow me."

Yet, paradoxically enough, Jesus, the preacher of disinterested love, talked very frequently of rewards. His promises form quite a considerable part of his gospel, so much so in fact that they furnish material for those modern ministers who specialize in the soothing comforts of the Christian

faith, making it a pious form of profit-taking.
The original gospel combination of challenge and
comfort is so often not presented in proper proportion by the pulpit interpreters. On the one
hand are those who flog the wills of their par-
ishioners without feeding their spirits; on the
other are those who give their flock an almost un-
broken diet "of boneless chicken stewed in
cream."

But the subtle paradox of Jesus' position shows
itself in the way he integrates the call for uncalculating service with the expectation of reward.
"If ye love them that love you, what reward have
ye?" (Matthew 5. 46). Here he uses the motive
of reward to rebuke the reciprocating type of love
which looks for return. And Luke elaborates the
same principle in reporting the statement: "If ye
lend to them of whom ye hope to receive, what
thank have ye? even sinners lend to sinners, to
receive again as much. But love your enemies,
and do them good, and lend, never despairing;
and your reward shall be great" (Luke 6. 34, 35).
Again the incentive of reward is used to inspire
disinterested action.

Of course one easy way around this paradox
would be by the route of heavenly reward. We
might explain it by saying that the followers of
Jesus were to forego earthly profit for the sake of
recompense in the life hereafter. Such future

payment after death is a familiar promise of traditional religion to the oppressed of earth. It is one
of the features of ecclesiasticism which has
brought it into popular disrepute in many quar-
ters. The idea of "pie in the sky, by and by" has
been incorporated by the proletariat into bitter
satirical song.

That Jesus did hold out the sustaining hope of
future reward is clear from several of his recorded
utterances. "Rejoice, and be exceeding glad: for
great is your reward in heaven" (Matthew 5. 12)
was the compensating comfort given to those
undergoing persecution for his sake. When he
commanded the wealthy young man to sell his
possessions and give to the poor, the promise was,
"thou shalt have treasure in heaven" (Mark 10.
21). It should be noted, however, that Jesus
used the hope of heavenly reward not as an opiate
to deaden men to the painful injustice of earth,
but as a stimulant to speed the coming of the
Kingdom and the doing of the divine will "as in
heaven so on earth" (Matthew 6. 10). But Jesus
did not limit his pledge of divine reward to the
days after death. When Peter heard Jesus'
promise of "treasure in heaven" to the rich young
man, he explicitly asked what was to be the reward
of the disciples who had left all to follow him.
In the Master's reply as given by Luke and
paralleled by Mark, he makes plain both the pres-

ent and future compensation. "There is no man
that hath left house, or wife, or brethren, or parents, or children, for the kingdom of God's sake,
who shall not receive manifold more in this time,
and in the world to come eternal life" (Luke 18.
29, 30). Hence we are faced with the paradox
that Jesus, the advocate of uncalculating love and
service, did hold before men the promise of
reward here in this life.

How can we reconcile this use of the profit motive to inspire disinterested effort? First of all,
it must be remembered that Jesus came to reveal
the love of God for man as well as to arouse the
love of man for God. How could he do justice
to the picture of a Heavenly Father unless he put
in the feature of his Fatherly generosity, his desire
to give good things to his children, exceeding the
eagerness of earthly parents to give to their off-
spring? Fatherhood involves keeping faith with
dutiful sons. To have omitted all reference to
divine rewards would have been to mutilate the
portrait of God.

Moreover, there is something other than self-
interest on man's part involved in this matter of
divine reward. Vital, human effort cannot be
sustained without the feeling that the work being
done is worth while. When physicians are trying
to restore the unstrung nerves of a mental case
in a sanatorium, it is necessary to assign tasks

which not only occupy the mind and hand, but which also give the feeling of usefulness. Every sane person wants to know whether his work has value. A Livingstone in Africa, a painter at his canvas, as well as a laborer in the ditch wishes to feel that his effort is worth while. To take away from men the belief in a God who guarantees values would be to cut the nerve of sustained endurance.

To ask about our work, "Does it pay?" is a sane and not necessarily selfish question. The unsocial elements creep in when we begin to ask such questions as "Does it pay me?" "How much does it pay?" "When does it pay?" Jesus tried to keep that distinction before the minds of his disciples. He would have them give themselves to their work, confident that God is a faithful guarantor of values. To this end he told them such parables as those of the talents and pounds. But Jesus would have them avoid that calculating attitude which keeps the eye on the personal reward and kills the spirit of loving service. To drive this home he used the illustration of the workers in the vineyard who received each the same, regardless of the hours employed. In linking this parable to his promise of reward he uses the enigmatical statement, "But many shall be last that are first; and first that are last" (Matthew 19. 30). And again at the close of the story Matthew

re-enforces this truth by an almost exact repetition. "So the last shall be first, and the first last"
(Matthew 20. 16).

This is the paradox which safeguards the principle of reward from killing the spirit of love.
This world, according to Jesus, is not a factory
wherein the wage agreements are all signed in
advance and the man who works for God gets his
pay envelope at the end of the day or the week.
This earth is not a department store wherein the
goods are all marked and ready for delivery upon
receipt of a stipulated payment. No, this is a
Father's house and we are the sons of God, not
bargaining but trusting. The followers of Jesus
are his fellow workers, not as servants putting in
time for a wage, but as friends putting in life for
love.

The rewards of God are not for the calculating
and cannot be mathematically calculated. Jesus
did not endorse the neat, dogmatic little explana-
tions of disasters or benefits as always sent by God
to punish or to reward individuals. When he
confronted a case of blindness and the bystanders
asked, "Who did sin, this man, or his parents, that
he should be born blind?" Jesus replied, "Neither
did this man sin, nor his parents" (John 9. 2, 3).
There are some cases of affliction which can be
clearly traced to the sufferer's misconduct, but not
all. Jesus the Physician would have men use all

precaution to push back the encroachments of pain, but despite all man's best efforts, disease does come. It is futile to flagellate the conscience, trying to interpret all our ailments as God's punishment for our sins.

Likewise there are calamities which cannot be explained as sent of God. When Jesus was told of the Galileans whose blood Pilate had mingled with their sacrifices, he said, "Think ye that these Galileans were sinners above all the Galileans, because they have suffered these things? I tell you, Nay. . . . Or those eighteen, upon whom the tower in Siloam fell, and killed them, think ye that they were offenders above all the men that dwell in Jerusalem? I tell you, Nay" (Luke 13. 2-5). Jesus did not join with Job's friends and their many modern successors who try to trace direct connections between disasters and the sins of the sufferers.

There are unpredictable and unpreventable calamities, such as earthquakes, cyclones, floods, and their like. Our legal terminology calls these "acts of God," and their causes do lie hidden in the laws of nature's God; but to say that an earthquake in San Francisco or a drought in Dakota is due to the excessive sinfulness of the dwellers in those places is unwarranted.

Similarly, earthly prosperity is not to be interpreted as always a mark of divine approval—an error which has too often aggravated the unsocial attitudes of Puritanism, even of all Christianity. The Heavenly Father "maketh his sun to rise on the evil and on the good, and sendeth rain on the just and the unjust" (Matthew 5. 45). Sometimes those who labor twelve hours seem to receive no more remuneration than those who toil only one hour. Often the last shall be first and the first last. There are incalculable, unpredictable, uncontrollable elements in life which defy attempts to decipher the divine pay roll.

This irregularity of reward creates a testing factor in the creation of character. It may make for weakness as well as for strength. On the one hand it unravels character when men count on the possibility of unearned divine bounty in lieu of prudence and preparation. It may beget a sort of gambling attitude toward God. When the gambling spirit gets into a man's blood, it drives out the red corpuscles of vigorous effort, unfits him for patient, sustained toil and causes the mind to lose its logical, step-by-step reasoning habits. This effect is to be seen in certain religious attitudes, masquerading piously as a devout, unquestioning trust in God. In a recent book, the head of an orphan school proudly boasted that many a week end found his institution with an empty larder, but his prayerful trust in God always brought the needed supplies by the next Monday.

Such hand-of-God to mouth-of-man existence may be a mark of the poor in spirit, but it is hardly the kind which was pronounced blessed by the Nazarene Leader who cautioned his disciples to sit down and count the cost before they started to follow him, lest they be like the builder who began to construct a tower and, unfortunately, could not finish it.

When the parable of the vineyard is set alongside the parable of the talents, it is clearly seen that Jesus was giving no encouragement to those who withhold their own efforts, counting either on the irregularity of the divine rewards or on the certainty of those rewards regardless of time employed. God's economy is no divine Townsend Plan, guaranteeing to the shiftless who will not try to provide for a future rainy day that the Lord will raise an umbrella large enough to cover them all. There is an old-age security in God's care but there is also an incentive to work in God's love. Like the lord of the vineyard, God pays according to the spirit of the workers, and be it noted that in the parable the first-hour laborers bargained for their wage while the later ones went in putting their trust in the promise of "Whatsoever is right."

The Lord of the harvest looketh upon the spirit of the sowers. That is the measure by which he appraises their work.

"All the world's coarse thumb
And finger failed to plumb
So passed in making up the main account;
All instincts immature
All purposes unsure
That told not as his work, but swelled
        the man's amount."

And to develop a spirit worthy of reward, these irregular and incalculable elements of life are necessary. Without them faith would not be called into play. Following after sure things involves no spirit of faith. The cautious, timid fellow who hid his talent in the earth lest he lose it, was not fit to receive a reward. In fact, "even that which he hath shall be taken away" (Matthew 25. 29). The farmer takes a chance when he puts his seed into the ground. Parents run a risk of heartbreak when they bring a child into the world. Love, the divinest thing in life, is fraught with the possibility of pain, sometimes burning with passion, sometimes aching with anxiety, sometimes freezing with despair. But these risks engender faith. Then, too, in confronting the unforeseen uncertainties of reward, men develop the qualities of patience, fortitude, and resourcefulness. The writer of Ecclesiastes expressed this when he said: "In the morning sow thy seed, and in the evening withhold not thy hand: for thou knowest not which shall prosper, whether this or that, or whether they both shall be alike good"

(Ecclesiastes 11. 6). The spirit of the farmer in taking his chance with the soil is far different from that of the gambler at the roulette table. The latter is breaking down his morale by counting on chance, whereas the farmer is building up his mental and moral strength by his efforts to conquer chance.

Moreover, the incalculable aspect of divine reward serves to foster the noncalculating spirit of genuine love. There could be no true love in a cut-and-dried world where rewards were guaranteed. Mother love would not be worthy of the name if it measured its care of children by the thought of what sons and daughters would do in return. Mothers give extra care to little crippled minds which can never repay. Sons would not be true sons if they meted out their devotion to parents on the basis of what they were going to get by inheritance. The fineness of filial love depends on how much it gives without thought of getting.

This would seem to be the particular point which Jesus was trying to drive home when he told the parable of the workers in the vineyard. That illustration was called forth by Peter's calculating, rather mercenary mood as reflected in his question as to what the disciples were to receive for their self-sacrificing service. Jesus was reminding Peter that work in the kingdom of God

must be performed in the spirit of trusting son-
ship and not of cold calculation. Whenever the
profit-seeking motive came to the fore among his
colleagues, Jesus sought to check it as in the case
of the mother of Zebedee's sons who asked that
they might have places of preferment in the Kingdom about to be established.

But when men do rise from the bargaining attitude to the spirit of faith and noncalculating love,
then they have reached a plane on which the laws
of divine reward are revealed as reliable and unfailing. In the realm of the spirit, it is true that
"whatsoever a man soweth, that shall he also reap"
(Galatians 6. 7). The farmer sowing his wheat
in the earth may not always get back his wheat,
but the spirit of patience and resourcefulness
which he puts into his work brings forth a harvest
of greater patience and resourcefulness. The
artist applying his interpretative powers to his
canvas may not receive adequate financial reward
for his effort, but he does acquire a greater power
of interpretation. The person pouring out his
loving service in behalf of another may not be
compensated by the reciprocating love of the
other, but he does develop a greater capacity for
love in himself. Thus "unto every one that hath
shall be given" (Matthew 25. 29). Given what?
More of that which he hath: if skill, more skill; if
fortitude, more fortitude; if love, more love. On

the level of the spirit, the laws of divine return
do hold good.

This spiritualization of reward explains the
enigmas of both the parable of the vineyard and
that of the talents. It was the spirit of the work-
men that was appraised and rewarded, and on that
basis the last were first. It was the spirit of courageous faith, shown by the five-talent and two-
talent servants, which called forth the commenda-
tion and received the increment. There is a law
of accumulation in the spiritual realm. Trust
begets more trust, courage expands courage.
"Unto everyone that hath shall be given." And
there is also a law of diminishing returns in the
realm of the spirit. The man of negative, timid
mind finds his resources being reduced by enervat-
ing, weakening suggestions. "From him that hath
not, even that which he hath shall be taken away."
Heaven and hell are but these laws of spiritual
addition and subtraction operating beyond the
grave.

This putting of divine rewards on the plane of
the spirit helps to clear up the popular confusion
concerning them. We often conclude that virtue
does not pay because we are looking for the payment on the material rather than on the spiritual
level. We often lose faith in the efficacy of prayer
because we watch for its answer in the wrong
place. If it is true that God is a Spirit and is to

be worshiped in spirit, does it not follow that we
should likewise expect answers to that worship to
come in and through the spirit? But we still look
for his rewards on the lower physical levels. We
put in our prayers to the God of the Spirit and
then expect to take out a cured body or a prosperous business or a bountiful crop down on the material level. These quick slot-machine methods of
expecting the rewards of prayer and virtue are
contrary to the teaching of Jesus and are bound
to beget disappointment.

To be sure, however, spiritual rewards do often
work through indirectly to manifest themselves in
the material realm. The prayers and service of
a good farmer do not change the weather but they
do increase his own resourcefulness and thereby
improve the crop. The health and peace of mind
begotten by prayer exert a curative effect on the
body "exceeding abundantly above all that we ask
or think, according to the power that worketh in
us." And while virtue is not always rewarded by
material prosperity, nevertheless the personal
moral qualities of good self-management do make
for mastery over physical surroundings.

In short, divine rewards reveal themselves
through a process of fertility rather than of quick
utility. Jesus suggested the distinction in his re-
marks after the woman had anointed him with
the precious perfume. The disciples complained

of the waste, saying, "This ointment might have been sold for much, and given to the poor" (Mat·thew 26. 9). But Jesus silenced their criticism, exclaiming, "Wheresoever this gospel shall be preached in the whole world, that also which this woman hath done shall be spoken of for a memorial of her" (Matthew 26. 13). It was as if Jesus were contrasting the quick utility of spending the money on the poor with the future fertilizing effect of the woman's uncalculating generosity as it would echo down the centuries, warming cold hearts, and causing the fruits of the spirit to grow. Some things which seem waste at the time enrich the soil for future production.

Divine rewards must be appraised in the light of this principle. The righteous man may not receive the prizes of the moment, but his very losses develop a richness in his life as it ripens toward maturity. Prayer and worship may seem a waste of time so far as the week's output is concerned, but in the long run they impart a resourcefulness and resiliency. A grain of wheat falling into the ground appears to decay but it is a death which gives birth to much fruit.

That is the principle by which the kingdom of God grows. That is the principle by which Jesus lived and died. Judged on the basis of immediate utility, Jesus' whole career seemed a series of bad bargains. He repeatedly gave more than he received. But Studdert-Kennedy catches the reflection of the spirit by which Jesus measured his work and sustained his morale when he describes the scene at the cross with the soldiers gambling for the garments of the crucified one:

"And sitting down they watched him there,
The soldiers did.
Then, while they played dice
He made his sacrifice.
And died upon the cross to rid
God's world of sin.
He was a gambler too,
My Christ.
He took his life and threw
It for a world redeemed.
And e'er his agony was done
Before the westering sun went down,
Crowning that day with its crimson crown,
He knew
That he had won."

CHAPTER XII

THE MAMMON OF RIGHTEOUSNESS

JESUS appeared utterly indifferent to money for his own use. There is no mention of what he earned as a carpenter, of what he received as a teacher, of what he spent as a traveler. Once in warning enthusiastic admirers from rashly joining his company, he reminded them that he was poorer than the foxes with their holes and the birds with their nests, for he had "not where to lay his head" (Matthew 8. 20). There may have been a note of sadness in that statement, but there was neither self-pity nor appeal for assistance. Jesus is never recorded as asking for alms, and the Gospels contain no treasurer's report.

But while Jesus seemed free from any personal concern about money, there is scarcely any subject to which he made more frequent reference. Being a realist, he recognized how the considerations of wealth are woven into the warp and woof of everyday living. As an heir of the Hebrew tradition he knew how material conditions were regarded as the measure of divine favor. National failure or success was looked upon by the Hebrews as the result of their relationship to Jehovah. "Doth

Job fear God for naught?" was the cynical Satanic way of putting the popular pre-Christian conception of religious devotion as a road to prosperity. It has been said that prosperity was the blessing of the Old Testament, and adversity the blessing of the New Testament.

Jesus came into an atmosphere charged with materialism. This accounts for the frequency of his lightning flashes on the subject of money. He saw that Mammon had become the very rival of God. And in the face of this rivalry the followers of Jesus must make a clear-cut choice of sovereignty. "Ye cannot serve God and mammon." The paradox appears, however, when Luke links this statement of Jesus with the counsel which goes before it: "Make to yourselves friends by means of the mammon of unrighteousness; that, when it shall fail, they may receive you into the eternal tabernacles" (Luke 16. 9). Mammon, the rival of God, is recommended as an aid on the road to God.

This single paradox only serves to climax the seeming contradictions which appear when certain of Jesus' various sayings on wealth are grouped together. "Lay not up for yourselves treasures upon the earth" (Matthew 6. 19), is a command which, if taken literally as a rule of life, would prohibit all accumulation of property. In line with that is Jesus' injunction to the rich young man, "Go, sell whatsoever thou hast, and give to the poor, and thou shalt have treasure in heaven" (Mark 10. 21). And sternly re-enforcing such statements is the assertion, "Whosoever he be of you that renounceth not all that he hath, he cannot be my disciple" (Luke 14. 33).

But, on the other hand, it would appear that Jesus accepted as associates in his enterprise some like Joanna, the wife of Herod's steward, and Susanna and "many others which ministered unto them of their substance" (Luke 8. 3). And Jesus could hardly have commanded Zacchaeus to renounce all that he had, as he did the rich young man, for when the prosperous publican announced that he would give half of his goods to the poor and repay fourfold what he had taken by false appraisal, the Master thereupon said, "Today is salvation come to this house" (Luke 19. 9). While Jesus so identified himself with the poor and underprivileged that whatsoever was done unto "one of the least of these" he felt to be done unto himself, nevertheless his parables often reflect the viewpoint of the employer and the landlord. This fact gives a certain credence to the contention of some commentators that in the carpenter shop at Nazareth Jesus was a master builder, an employer rather than an employee. At least, it may be said that the distinction between the employing and the employed was not so clearly and technically drawn in Jesus' day as in ours, and the line of demarcation is dim in the Gospels. In view of these apparently conflicting statements, what was Jesus' position on property? When he spoke, there were times in which his hearers marveled at his practical wisdom; there were other times at which they deemed him a dreaming fool. Now that his reported utterances are fixed in the record, some of them are selected by the Communists as the basis for claiming Jesus as their comrade; others are taken by Wall Street executives as shrewd precepts making for bigger and better business.[1]

When Jesus sheds his light on the manifold subject of money, that light seems to break up into all the colors of the spectrum. Out of it all some things became clear. The first is that Jesus was not essaying to formulate a formal set of economic rules. In this matter of property we see more concretely than almost anywhere else his fundamental practice of speaking in terms of principles rather than of rules. It has been suggested that Jesus' silence on economic and certain other subjects can be explained by his statement that he had many other things to say unto his disciples which they could not bear at that time (John 16. 12). But it seems more nearly true to the temper of Jesus to say that he deliberately pre-

[1] Compare Bruce Barton, *The Man Nobody Knows.*

ferred to leave his teaching in this matter on the plane of principles. Economic formulas which fit the comparatively simple situations of the first century would have been outmoded in a machine age. Principles persist. Modern proponents of economic plans may claim Jesus' support for their motives but they can hardly enroll him in their membership or put his label on their elaborated programs.

A second fact revealed in the Gospels is, that Jesus did not prescribe for classes as classes. There was little of the class agitator about the Nazarene Carpenter. Here we must take issue with the implications of Professor Macmurray when he says: "It is one of the less recognized characteristics of the story of Jesus as we find it in the Gospels that his attitude to members of the ruling class is one of mistrust and hostility. His manner when dealing with members of the common people is very different and full of that sympathy and tenderness which is such an outstanding feature of his personal relationships. And while it is perhaps true that he never attacked with bitterness any individual, it is also true that his class attacks are almost unrivaled in literature for the bitterness of their invective."[2] To prove his contention that Jesus was antagonistic to the wealthy as a class, Macmurray cites the Master's

[2] *Creative Society*, p. 50. Eddy and Page.

curt reception of the rich young man. This would seem a rather unfortunate bit of evidence to offer, for Mark explicitly states with regard to the young scion of wealth, "and Jesus looking upon him, loved him" (Mark 10. 21).

To be sure, Jesus did denounce the rich Pharisees who made pious prayers and then devoured widows' houses. And he did scathingly rebuke the self-seeking and social climbing which he witnessed in the homes of his wealthy hosts, where guests sought the best seats and those were invited who could repay the hospitality. But he also in drawing an analogy implied a rebuke to the servant who would expect an extra reward for doing only what it was his duty to do (Luke 17. 7-10). Jesus saw that the sins of greed and covetousness run through all strata of society, and consequently he sought to remove them from the disinherited brother who asked that his inheritance might be recovered (compare Luke 12. 13), as well as from the rich young man who refused to give up his possessions.

Jesus realized that classless sins cannot be cured by class legislation or share-the-wealth schemes. His kinship of interest was with the poor, and the inequalities of economic status cut him to the quick. It was not, therefore, lack of sympathy which prompted him in the case of the disinherited brother to exclaim, "Who made me a

judge or a divider over you?" But it was his realization that a mere redistribution of property
would not eradicate the covetous motives which
are the causes of recurring economic evils. Jesus
dug more deeply to the roots of sin than do some
of our modern economic reformers.

To do this, he avoided blunderbuss broadsides
against such vague general targets as humanity,
the masses, the bourgeois, the proletariat. He
individualized his applications into such cases as
those of a rich shortsighted farmer, a self-indul-
gent unsympathetic Dives, a vineyard owner and
his laborers. And while Jesus is reported as having indulged in one notable general invective
against the ruling Pharisee class, he did not count
on blanket group indictments to bring personal
conviction of sin.

A third implication in Jesus' teaching regarding wealth is that the right of holding property
privately carries the duty of using it socially. He
seemed to take for granted the right of private
property. His repeated injunctions to charity
would imply personal ownership, for without possessions one cannot give alms. In his parable of
the great supper, he cited the excuses given by
certain invited guests. One said, "I have bought
a field, and I must needs go out and see it." Another said, "I have bought five yoke of oxen, and
I go to prove them" (Luke 14. 18, 19). Jesus

rebuked the making of these excuses but he did not raise the issue of the right to own the field and the oxen. The evil in the situation lay in the fact that personal concern with such secondary things prevented acceptance of the great social purposes of the kingdom of God. In the parable of the pounds Jesus also appeared to recognize without question the nobleman's right to the property which he divided.

And as to the social use of wealth, it should be remembered that in Jesus' day about the only recognized means was the giving of alms. The modern distinction between the private ownership of the processes of consumption and the public ownership of the means of production, did not appear over the horizon of the Gospels. While it may be that the parable of the vineyard workers reveals the principle of the minimum living wage in the mind of Jesus, and while other economic legislative principles may have been present in embryo, the Nazarene Carpenter did not enter into the questions of taxation and State control of wealth. When an attempt was made by framing an adroit question to involve him in the political issue of Roman taxation, he contented himself and disconcerted his critics by saying simply, "Render therefore unto Caesar the things that are Caesar's; and unto God the things that are God's" (Matthew 22. 21).

But if our social expectations of Jesus at first seem disappointed by his avoidance of concrete prescriptions, let us note a fourth feature of his teaching on wealth, namely, that charitable use does not make up for unrighteous accumulation. The giving of alms and the payment of tithes are not satisfactory substitutes for leaving undone "the weightier matters of the law, justice, and mercy, and faith" (Matthew 23. 23). The odor of sanctity in giving does not take out the taint of corruption in making. Justice and brotherhood come before charity and altar sacrifices. "If therefore thou art offering thy gift before the altar, and there rememberest that thy brother hath aught against thee, leave there thy gift before the altar, and go thy way, first be reconciled to thy brother, and then come and offer thy gift" (Matthew 5. 23-25).

If it be said that Jesus in suggesting social uses of money did not go much beyond the encouragement of charity, it should be added that he projected the implications of charitableness into the whole motivation of economic life. A sensitive regard for personality was, as we have seen, the touchstone of all his ethics. Property, like the Sabbath, was made for man and not man for property. The payment of the laborers in the vineyard was proportioned according to the personal elements involved rather than according to the grapes picked. Jesus was interested in making men, not money or things.

A fifth ray in the light which Jesus shed on wealth was the peril of its possession. While it is true that the sins of greed and covetousness poison the minds of the poor as well as the rich, it is nevertheless a fact that wealth, like an intoxicant, tends to strengthen its grip on man's spirit. Greed usually grows with possessions. Wealth also has a way of blinding its owners to the presence of the needy, even of the beggars at the gate. It dulls the social insight, as in the case of the rich young man, causing him to be content with the virtues of personal decency without vital concern for the welfare of others. Wealth has a tendency to drug men into an increasing dependence on itself until the acquisitive impulses become so swollen and bloated that "it is easier for a camel to go through the eye of a needle than for a rich man to enter into the kingdom of God" (Mark 10. 25). Possessions beget a false sense of security, and men, like the farmer with his bounteous crops, go on building barns and laying up treasure on the earth oblivious of the approach of death.

So pervasive is this peril of wealth that it rises into rivalry with God. To denote its demonic power Jesus uses an Aramaic expression, "Mammon," in a semi-personified sense. And the sixth ray in Jesus' financial spectrum is the sovereignty of God over Mammon. The tension of trying to serve both is too great for efficiency in the service of either. "No servant can serve two masters: for either he will hate the one, and love the other; or else he will hold to one, and despise the other" (Luke 16. 13). Herein lies the trouble of many who call themselves Christians. They have just enough allegiance to God to make them uncomfortable when they are serving Mammon, and not enough to make them comfortable when they turn from Mammon to God.

In contrast with this divided loyalty Jesus cited the illustration of the unscrupulous steward who reduced the debts of his employer's customers in order to secure their aid in finding a new position for himself. Despite his dishonesty, the fellow showed a commendable singleness of purpose. The steward served only Mammon and thereby manifested a wisdom greater than "the sons of light" with their divided allegiance and weakened efficiency. "Ye cannot serve God and mammon."

This leads us to a seventh aspect of Jesus' teaching on wealth, namely, that once mammon can be demoted from its status as a rival of God, it can become the servant of God. Jesus' primary purpose was the perfection of human personality. Toward this end Jesus proceeded by the principle of athleticism rather than of asceticism. He might have commanded his followers ascetically to eschew all possible contacts with material possessions. But there is a certain anaemic quality developed in the ascetic. Jesus, on the other hand, desired not that his disciples be taken out of the world, but that they should be kept from the evil one (John 17. 15). He would have them remain in the midst of life's actualities to wrestle with its problems, and risk its hazards, thereby developing toughness of moral fiber and fullness of spiritual stature.

Mammon is one of the worldly factors to be mastered and used rather than avoided. "Make to yourselves friends by means of the mammon of unrighteousness; that, when it shall fail, they may receive you into the eternal tabernacles" (Luke 16. 9). Just as the dishonest steward through the use of money made friends for his temporal future, so the followers of Jesus by their handling of money are to make those friendships which insure an eternal future. Men may use their material possessions as means of developing those qualities of character which survive the moth and rust of earthly treasure.

Wealth, said Jesus, is a training ground in trusteeship. By fidelity to their property trusts men fit themselves for possessing "the true riches" (Luke 16. 10-12). Money is the nerve of generosity and may serve as the muscle to extend and strengthen it. Wealth, which has a natural tendency to limit sympathy, may work to enlarge it, by sending forth treasure which draws the heart after it, for "where thy treasure is there shall thy heart be also"—a principle which works in the kingdom of heaven here as well as hereafter. Fidelity, sympathy, generosity—these and their like are the "true riches" of life which last on into the eternal tabernacles.

Jesus could have reduced the tension of discipleship by advocating an ascetic avoidance of money. A vow of poverty puts less continuous strain on a person than does a truly Christian handling of property. But Jesus did not simplify living by demanding poverty of all. Nor did he urge an absolute equality of wealth. In the perfection of personality men must use ingenuity and imagination, discrimination and judgment, progressive sympathy and sacrifice. Nothing tests these more than does the mastering of mammon. But when mastered, mammon, the rival of God, becomes the servant to God.

CHAPTER XIII

THE PRUDENCE IN PROVIDENCE

WHEN Jesus was at the height of his popularity, he turned one day to the crowd following him and dampened their enthusiasm with the dash of a cold calculating question. He bade them pause and consider the prospect of accompanying him. "Which of you, desiring to build a tower, doth not first sit down and count the cost, whether he have wherewith to complete it? Lest haply, when he hath laid a foundation, and is not able to finish, all that behold begin to mock him, saying, This man began to build and was not able to finish" (Luke 14. 28-30). No business man could have spoken with more practical prudence.

But what executive would send out representatives of his firm with the counsel which Jesus gave to his disciples on their early mission of healing and teaching: "Get you no gold, nor silver, nor brass in your purses; no wallet for your journey, neither two coats, nor shoes, nor staff" (Matthew 10. 9, 10). "For the laborer is worthy of his hire" (Luke 10. 7). "But when they deliver you up, be not anxious how or what ye shall speak: for it shall be given you in that hour what ye shall speak" (Matthew 10. 19). Worldly wisdom would certainly term such instruction a foolhardy trust in Providence.

Or turn to Jesus' parable of the unscrupulous steward and note how he praised the fellow's foresight as superior to that of the "sons of light." From the illustration Jesus pointed the need of more shrewd and practical planning on the part of his followers. But contrast this call to look ahead with his sweeping words against worrying over the tomorrows. "Be not therefore anxious, saying, What shall we eat? or, What shall we drink? or, Wherewithal shall we be clothed? . . . Be not therefore anxious for the morrow: for the morrow will be anxious for itself" (Matthew 6. 31, 34).

What did Jesus advocate, an enlightened prudence or an uncalculating trust in Providence? We can hardly get around the seemingly paradoxical contradictions of his statements by merely saying that Jesus stood for prudence in spiritual matters and trusted Providence in material affairs. Jesus was too realistic to departmentalize life in that fashion. He saw that man does "not live by bread alone," but also that he cannot live without bread. He himself gave bread to the hungry. He was concerned about man's material welfare as an integral part of what he called life. Hence we must look more deeply into his attitude toward Providence and prudence.

Jesus clearly was an advocate of preparedness. His own career shows the strategy of planning, even of change in plans. Whether he was drawn with the crowd to hear John the Baptist or whether he chose that moment of popular religious fervor to launch his public ministry, we do not know. But it was a strategic hour. And before he began his campaign of healing and teaching, he withdrew into the wilderness to formulate his principles and methods of work. His first ministry was in Galilee, away from the center of ecclesiastical and political leadership which would have scotched his enterprise before it got under way. When he had aroused the interest of his countrymen, he moved on the capital city, where the crucial issues had to be focused. He chose his time of spectacular entrance at the Passover season when Jerusalem would be full of pilgrims, and, according to the record, he designed and planned his entry with prophetic insight and foresight. The journeys of Jesus were no aimless wandering. They show the genius of generalship.

Jesus was no opportunist, waiting for providential circumstance to turn something up. He seems to have taken certain practical forethought for the physical needs of his company inasmuch as he had a designated treasurer. He timed his strokes and his teaching. The fourth Gospel records Jesus as countering his disciples' urge to make an early visit to Jerusalem with the reply, "My time is not yet come" (John 7. 6). And the first Gospel interprets him as making preparations for his final Passover with the words, "My time is at hand" (Matthew 26. 18).

This fitting into a time schedule was not the attitude of fatalism. Jesus does not picture himself as a pawn drawn across the chessboard of Palestine in order to win a divine game of salvation. He recognized a divine plan and necessity but not in such a way as to preclude personal freedom. "Woe unto the world because of occasions of stumbling! for it must needs be that the occasions come; but woe to that man through whom the occasion cometh!" (Matthew 18. 7.) The necessity of Jesus' death did not remove the blame from Judas as if he were a helpless tool, nor did it rob Jesus of the virtue of voluntary sacrifice. The Master's timing of his program had in it the elements of choice and prevision.

Moreover, his parables encouraged the virtues of thrift and foresight. The wise virgins were those with sufficient prudence to provide oil for a possible delay. The commended servant was the faithful one whom his master, on his return, found watching over the household (Matthew 24. 46).

The wise master of the house was he who guarded against the coming of the thief in the night. Jesus' repetition of the words "ready" and "watch" is ample refutation of the charge that he advocated a blind trust in Providence.

And while he did send his disciples forth on their early practice deputation without purse and without preparation as to what they should say in case they were haled into court, nevertheless he counseled a certain prudence. "I send you forth as sheep in the midst of wolves: be ye therefore wise as serpents, and harmless as doves" (Matthew 10. 16). There was to be no foolish inviting of needless opposition, no blind sheepish stumbling into difficulties. Jesus saw that the work of the Kingdom can be hindered quite as much by the sheepishness of the sheep as by the wolfishness of the wolves. His followers were to expect persecution and be brave in the face of it, but they were to "beware of men" and not open themselves to futile suffering. Jesus called for courage but not reckless bravado.

In line with Jesus' habit of preparedness was his final instruction to his disciples as reported by Luke. "Tarry ye in the city, until ye be clothed with power from on high" (Luke 24. 49). Here was precaution against premature action. Although they had been witnesses of his works and were now trustees of his program, they were not

to rush rashly into action until they had the power
to be effective. This "power from on high" was
the crowning element of Christlike preparedness.

In Jesus' foresight there was the element of
prudence, but it was large rather than petty.
There is a prudence that is small; there is also
a prudence that is large. There is the foresight
of the sheep which as it nibbles the grass looks a
few feet ahead to the green blade and noses its
way toward it, frightened at the slightest sound
yet frequently wandering into pitfalls. There is
also the foresight of the eagle which sees its food
and its danger from the distant crag and wheels
its course in wide circles. There is the prudence
of the peasant who thriftily stores his coins under
the floor in preparation for a future rainy day.
There is the prudential foresight of a James J.
Hill who sees the possibilities of a vast Northwest
and threads it with his railroads. There is the
cautious prudence of the timid person who tip-
toes toward every opportunity with his favorite
maxim, "A bird in the hand is worth two in the
bush." There is also the farsighted prudence of
the Pilgrim Fathers who gave up their securities
in the hand on the shores of Holland, that they
might seek something more in the bushes of the
American wilderness.

What Jesus sought to do was to lift men from
the petty prudence of miserly living to the long

foresights of the abundant life. When he said, "Be not anxious for the morrow," he was not telling his followers to close their eyes to the future, but to look further ahead than the immediate tomorrows. The novice at the wheel of a motor car tends to look at objects in the too near foreground, with the result that he steers nervously and uncertainly. The experienced driver levels out his gaze with a larger look ahead and thereby lessens the strain in himself and steadies the course of his car. Jesus advocated a foresight which delivers men from the immediacy, tension, and anxiety of shortsightedness.

When he confronted the cautious spirits that were waiting to see the outcome of his enterprise before investing their lives in it, Jesus told the parable of the talents, in which disgrace fell on the fellow who hid his talent because he was afraid to trust it in circulation. His was a petty prudence which fell short even of thrift. There is no implication that those who gained the extra talents were reckless speculators. They were praised as having been faithful to a lord who expected an increment in his investment. Fidelity to trust requires foresight and thrift.

Again, it was a lengthening of foresight which Jesus encouraged in his parable of the rich farmer. That benighted fellow could not see beyond his barns. He had so come to live and move and have his being in material things that he did not look to the ultimate ownership of his possessions. Jesus would have men lift their eyes to the question of what it is to be "rich toward God" (Luke 12. 21). It is the Master of the long view who asks, "What shall a man be profited, if he shall gain the whole world, and forfeit his life? or what shall a man give in exchange for his life?" (Matthew 16. 26.)

Now, of course, to the man of petty prudential type the methods of the larger prudence often seem extravagant and wasteful. When Henry Ford and his early associates divided their first profits in the automobile industry, he was advised to invest his share of the dividends in something safe and stable rather than to risk it in the hazardous uncertainties of making motors. But Ford counted on a longer future. Similarly, when the popular Teacher and Physician of Galilee announced his intention of investing his life in a cross, his outspoken disciple Peter tried to restrain him. But the same foresight which beheld Peter the rock in Simon the shifting, looked ahead and saw salvation in a cross. Jesus' larger prudence was willing to risk the seed corn for the "much fruit" of the harvest. Like Gladstone in the hour of Parliamentary defeat, Jesus was buoyed up with the belief that time was on his side. And while some of his injunctions may be colored by the current apocalyptic expectation of a near end of the era, his basic attitude is better explained by the fact that he counted on a larger future than did his contemporaries.

Thus Jesus' long foresight was based on his belief in a co-operating and continuing Providence. In this he struck a note not popularly held in his day. "The first century B. C. is an exceptionally depressing age. Good men succumbed to melancholy; others regarded the world as a bad jest. To the Stoic thinker Providence invariably contains a hint, and more than a hint, of unseeing implacable Fate. The predominating Stoic temper is that, not of joyful trust in God but of sad, brave resignation, coupled at times with a lofty self-righteousness."[1] Jesus, however, did not see nature as "red in tooth and claw." He viewed the world so realistically that he concluded only a cross could cure its sins. But withal it was a Father's world, not an arena presided over by an unfeeling Fate. And to the faithful he held out the promise, "Fear not, little flock; for it is your Father's good pleasure to give you the kingdom" (Luke 12. 32).

Jesus pictured God not as a Deity waiting passively to be found by men, but as a Father seeking his lost children. The prodigal's parent was

---

[1] H. R Mackintosh, *The Originality of the Christian Message,* pp. 69, 70, Duckworth & Co.

out on the road running to meet the returning sinner. The Heavenly Father to whom the followers of Jesus pray is one who knoweth what they have need of and is eager to give good things to his children. The kingdom of heaven is not an organization created by man but an organism born of God to be appropriated by men.

At times Jesus suggests that appropriation is in the nature of a welcome, "like unto men looking for their lord, when he shall return from the marriage feast; that, when he cometh and knocketh, they may straightway open unto him" (Luke 12. 36). This is the conception caught and repeated by the writer of Revelation when he interprets the spirit of the Lord as saying, "Behold, I stand at the door and knock: if any man hear my voice and open the door, I will come in to him, and will sup with him, and he with me" (Revelation 3. 20). Or, translated from personal into physical terms, God's activity moves toward man as the earth's fertility inclines itself toward the seed placed in the ground.

But the appropriation of providential power requires more than passive receptivity on the part of man. Man must work his way to meet the co-operation of God. "Not every one that saith unto me, Lord, Lord, shall enter into the kingdom of heaven; but he that doeth the will of my Father which is in heaven" (Matthew 7. 21). Jesus gave more emphasis to man's part in salvation than did some of the early exponents of his gospel and some of their present-day successors. The Christian combination of divine and human activity is reflected in Paul's paradoxical counsel to the Philippians: "Work out your own salvation with fear and trembling; for it is God which worketh in you both to will and to work" (Philippians 2. 12, 13). Or, to use a crude analogy, the co-ordination of man with divine power is somewhat like the blending of human effort with the buoyancy of the water in the act of swimming. The beginner when tossed into the water feels that he must do everything himself, and consequently he threshes and splashes with tense violence, whereas the experienced swimmer trusts himself to the supporting water with a lithe and easy grace. Jesus, to put it simply, was a superb swimmer in the waters of life.

It was at this point that the difference may be seen between Jesus and John the Baptist. The latter was an heroic figure, fearless preacher of righteousness, unbending upholder of moral standards, ascetic follower of lofty ideals. But when John in his enforced prison retirement became impatient at the progress Jesus was making, the Master uttered his enigmatical appraisal of the great forerunner. He said, "Among them that are born of women there hath not arisen a

greater than John the Baptist: yet he that is but
little in the kingdom of heaven is greater than he.
And from the days of John the Baptist until now
the kingdom of heaven suffereth violence" (Matthew 11. 11, 12).   John, great as he was, missed
the secret of Kingdom entrance.

The Baptist knew how to work for God, but he
had not learned how to wait for God.   He did his
duty grimly, but he did not succeed in entering
into the joyous confidence and radiant satisfaction of the Jesus way.   He never reached the point
where he felt the lift of his faith.   He was like an
airplane that taxies furiously ahead but does not
rise from the ground.   He worked for God without letting God work sufficiently with and for
him.   In that sense "he that is but little in the
kingdom" had something John missed.

There is a point at which human effort, if
persevered in, releases the power of divine aid.
This principle of release is similar to that seen in
music.   Piano lessons are a visible effort on the
part of most youthful novitiates.   But the study of
music pursued past a certain point begins to take
hold of the pupil and he is held to it by the attraction of his art.   So is it with the act of giving.   At
first thought most persons do not really appreciate
the truth of the saying, "It is more blessed to give
than to receive."   At least the faces of the average
congregation do not light up with pleasure when

the minister repeats the statement before taking up the collection. The blessing of giving is an acquired one. The makers of financial appeals have a bromidic way of saying, "Give until it hurts." On that basis charity would stop quite short with many persons. But the New-Testament counsel would be, "Give until it stops hurting," for there is a point beyond which the displeasure of letting go is transformed into the pleasure of generosity.

Similarly, in our religious attitudes, effort after awhile begins to feel itself supplemented by "a power from on high." Many do not persist until they release this lifting power. They have gone just far enough to make them feel an uncomfortable strain when they cling to worldly things and not enough to make them feel the buoyancy of godliness. Jesus left with his disciples the prescription to tarry in Jerusalem, the unpleasant place where their fortitude would be tested by the popular hatred of their crucified Leader. They held on, and Pentecost did come. When men tarry in their Jerusalems, holding on past their wits' end, they touch forces with "him that is able to do exceeding abundantly above all that we ask or think, according to the power that worketh in us" (Ephesians 3. 20).

Jesus counted on this "Power not ourselves that makes for righteousness." This trust gave to his life a rhythm between action and prayer. It lengthened his foresight beyond the factors which logic could see in any situation. Jesus held that men are workers together with God, a living Heavenly Father. Since they work with a living Being they should count on his progressive action as well as their own. Jesus would not have his followers therefore withhold action until reason can see through beyond the shadow of a doubt. He would have them start while the shadows of doubt may be thick upon them. But walking with God they find ways opening before them. "Seek first the kingdom of God," and the main current of life will take care of the eddies. Thus the larger prudence envisages a trustworthy providence.

CHAPTER XIV

THE TRUSTFUL FEAR

MACAULAY said of the Puritans that "they feared nothing but God." That same distinction might seem to explain the differentiation which Jesus made in the objects of fear. "Be not afraid of them which kill the body, but are not able to kill the soul: but rather fear him which is able to destroy both soul and body in hell" (Matthew 10. 28; compare Luke 12. 4, 5). It is a well-known experience that a great fear can drive out lesser fears from our minds. A man, for instance, may be coming home from his work filled with the worries of business. He is greeted at the door with the news that a member of his family has just met with a serious accident which threatens her life. Immediately the anxieties of business disappear in the shadow of the new fear. May it be that Jesus was trying thus to supplant our fears of men with the fear of God?

The ease and simplicity of such an explanation are complicated, however, by the context in both Matthew and Luke. In each Gospel account, this call to fear God is followed by the call to trust God. "Are not two sparrows sold for a farthing? and not one of them shall fall on the ground with-

131

out your Father: but the very hairs of your head are all numbered. Fear not therefore; ye are of more value than many sparrows" (Matthew 10. 29-31). This is anything but a picture of a God to inspire fear. Jesus has put his danger signal of divine fear against a background of divine fatherliness. The paradox of Jesus is that he counsels a fear begotten of trust in God.

When we study the records, we find that there was nothing which Jesus felt called upon to challenge more frequently than fear. He saw that fear hounded his friends from birth to death and drove them like frightened animals into all sorts of pitfalls. He observed that fear blinded the minds of men, making them unable to look facts in the face or trust themselves to truth. He found that fear paralyzed men's faculties, poisoned their emotions, and sapped their bodies. Jesus realized that if there was to be any genuine mastery of life, there must be a better control of fear.

He himself was the master of his own fears. No one ever saw the back of Jesus turned in fear. When he was struck, he did not strike back, but there was something about his look that showed that he was not restrained by mere fear. When Pilate had him in court, the Roman governor thought his prisoner a fool, but he did not think him a coward. There were no sudden dangers which shook his poise. There were no crises which shattered his nerve. Perhaps nothing helped more to win for Jesus the title of Master than did his superb control of fear.

Hence it would be hard to find in all the New Testament a statement more characteristic of Jesus than the command, "Fear not," or, as Weymouth puts it, "Away with fear." To locate these words would be to give a road-map of the Gospels. When the worried multitudes came out to hear him on the mount, he said, "Be not anxious" (Matthew 6. 25). To his frightened followers on a storm-tossed vessel his word was, "It is I; be not afraid" (Matthew 14. 27). In the house of mourning it is again the same assurance of faith, "Fear not, only believe" (Mark 5. 37). At the Last Supper, when he with his friends was looking into the shadow of his own grave, still it is the same message of courage, "Let not your heart be troubled; neither let it be fearful" (John 14. 27). The Man of Nazareth, who himself was never called a coward, went about trying to fortify his friends for their hours of crisis. No counsel came more often from his lips than "Fear not."

Jesus' endeavor to deliver men from fear had several phases. First of all, he sought to reawaken the spontaneous trustfulness of childhood. The normal healthy mind of the child is not clouded with suspicions, nor are its wings of imagination and faith clipped by complexes and calculations.

But the "trailing clouds of glory" which accompany childhood on its way from "God who is our home" are replaced all too soon by the misty shadows of distrust which attend our so-called worldly wisdom. Jesus would deliver our adult minds from the dominion of our distrusts by having them reborn. When he looked into the "cabined, cribbed, confined" soul of a calculating Nicodemus, he saw that liberation could come by nothing less than being "born again." That Pharisee teacher's mind would have to cut loose from its moorings of class consciousness and social consideration and become as free as the wind "which bloweth where it listeth." Such fearless freedom is the characteristic of "every one that is born of the Spirit" (John 3. 8).

This rebirth restores what Paul says God gave us, "not a spirit of fearfulness; but of power and love and discipline" (2 Timothy 1. 7). Such healthy-mindedness is a preventive against the infection of fear. It makes the spirit immune to germs of suspicion. It puts one on that high-minded plane of thought to which anxieties low-born of envy and pettiness cannot climb. This health of mind protects us from the jolts of life as the pneumatic tire cushions the car against the jar of the road. And, like the tire, the spirit is the more easily injured when the pressure is low. When our vitality is low, any little sharpness will

puncture our serenity. Realizing this, Jesus made
the cultivation of a healthy, sound, affirmative
mind as the first factor in conquering fear.

He tried to impart this to his followers in advance of the frightening experience. Dr. William
Abernethy tells of taking his watch to a jeweler,
who advised him that a delicate timepiece, if it
is carried on the person, should be wound in the
morning rather than at night. "For," said the
jeweler, "the watch suffers many shocks as its
owner moves about and it should start the day on
a strong spring." Similarly, Jesus would have his
disciples start the day on "a strong spring." He
fortified their courage in advance by morning
solitude and prayer before the crowds beset them,
by the intimate, soul-quickening comradeship of
a Last Supper before the arrest and trial, by Gethsemane before Calvary.

Jesus imparted this fortifying healthy-mindedness as a wise physician does. The fourth Gospel
illustrates the method of the Master in the case
of the woman at Jacob's Well. She was one
against whom the doors of decent society had been
shut, and in retaliation she had closed the doors
of her life against the socially respectable. Shut
into herself, she was breathing over and over her
suspicions and slights, her dislikes and distrusts,
until the windows of her mind were filmed with
self-generated fears. When Jesus entered into

her situation, his influence was like that of a cheering doctor in a shadowy room of sickness, where the patient is magnifying her symptoms. The Master conveyed to her such an invigorating spirit of trust that she overcame her unsocial attitude and went forth summoning the Samaritans.

Jesus fortified his disciples against dispiriting fear as a coach injects courage into a football squad. When his little company had suffered so many reverses and defections that one more loss threatened to put them in panic, their Leader said to them, "Fear not, little flock; for it is your Father's good pleasure to give you the kingdom" (Luke 12. 32). Like a good trainer, Jesus did not merely try to shake his players out of their defeatism by slaps of challenge or pats of encouragement. He built up their morale with a diet of hope and trust. A fainting person may be revived by a dash of cold water, but anaemia cannot be cured by repeated dashes of cold water. The blood content must be built up. Jesus did not endeavor to shock men into salvation but tried to develop them into the health of mind and fullness of stature characteristic of the abundant life.

Unlike so many evangelists, Jesus did not have any sin obsession. Incomparably sensitive to sin, he did not allow the evils around him to monopolize the foreground of his mind. The focus of his

thought was on the potential goodness rather than
the apparent badness of men.

Unlike most moralists, Jesus did not proceed
on the primary principle of making men ashamed
of themselves. Shame is a matrix of fear. The
fourth Gospel reflects the spirit of Jesus, however the actual record may be questioned, in the
case of the adulterous woman. When the crushed
and broken spirit of the Magdalene was brought
before him, he did not add to the shame already
heaped upon her, but he lifted her with a restorative belief in herself. "Neither do I condemn
thee: go thy way; from henceforth sin no more"
(John 8. 11). Herein Jesus was demonstrating
the spirit of the "chosen servant" described by
Isaiah and ascribed by Matthew to the Nazarene:

"A bruised reed shall he not break
And smoking flax shall he not quench"
(Matthew 12. 20).

What was said of Jane Addams could be applied
to Jesus. He "inhabited reality." He was a realist. He saw life from the shadow of a cross, and
nothing can be more realistic than that. But the
shadow of the cross did not dim his vision. It
only sharpened it for the sunny vistas. Jesus'
view penetrated to the very symptoms of sin. He
saw the poisoned sources in the imagination. He
experienced the desertion of neighbors, the fal-

sity of friends, the venomous spittle of the crowd,
the crucifying pains of suborned justice. But he
did not behold the sum of these ugly aspects and
say with the cynics, "That's human nature." Jesus
balanced his picture of man's brutalities and
bestialities with the fidelity of fathers, the trustfulness of little children, the loyalty of servants,
the suffering sympathy of friends. These too are
"human nature." In fact, the totality of impression gained from reading the records of Jesus is
not the depravity of man, but the possible redemp-
tion of man. Jesus banked on the gold in human
nature. He died hoping, not hopeless.

This fundamental confidence in the world as a
Father's house and in man as the child of God was
Jesus' basis of approach to the problem of fear.

Then, too, Jesus sought to deliver men from the
fears which rise out of the past. He realized that
the yelping pack of yesterday's hounding anxieties are so prone to break in upon today's peace of
mind. To counteract this, Jesus taught the principle of closing the mental gates in the rear. In
part this was but a technique of executive efficiency. When he said, "No man, having put his
hand to the plow, and looking back, is fit for the
kingdom of God" (Luke 9. 62), Jesus was enunci-
ating a principle whose practical value is apparent to anyone who has experienced the distrac-
tions of regret and remorse. These last have a

paralyzing effect. And the man of action must form the habit of shutting the door on what has been and cannot be undone. He must free himself from the futile and wearying practice of retracing the steps by which he reached yesterday's decision and wondering whether he might have done them differently. As a leader of men, Jesus therefore commanded, "Eyes front!"

But this deliverance from rearward fears is to be effected by something more than human effort and habit. Jesus stressed the truth of divine forgiveness. God's forgiving love transforms remorse into repentance. Remorse is the attitude of looking regretfully and hopelessly back at past misdeeds. Repentance is seeing the evil passed as the driver sees in his mirror the perils on the road behind him, from which he has been delivered. Remorse turns its face toward the past; repentance turns its back on it. Remorse feels the frightening clutch of the bad that has been done; repentance feels the releasing freedom of God who "breaks the power of cancelled sin."

Thus by the control of the backward look, Jesus would free men from the fears rising out of the past. Furthermore, by the use of the upward look he sought to deliver men from the fears of the present. Jesus realized how easily human beings became slaves of convention and victims of the curse of comparisons. Back of his injunction not to be anxious about "what ye shall eat, or what ye shall drink; nor yet for your body, what ye shall put on" (Matthew 6. 25), was the Master's understanding how these daily dreads arise. He knew that much of his hearers' anxiety arose not from the fear of actual starvation, but from the dread of not being able to keep up with the living standards around them. Hence Jesus shrewdly, perhaps with a twinkle in his eye, said, "Behold the birds of the heaven." They were to take their eyes off their neighbors' creations and look up at God's creatures.

When we earth-bound spirits do look up at the birds of the heaven, we awaken to the realization that we are not trying to keep up with their simple needs, but with our artificial social standards. Men have a way of putting it colloquially, "We must keep in the swim," which means, not that they are afraid of drowning, but that they wish to look as well as their neighbors on the beach. Jesus saw how many of our anxieties are born of pride, not of need, of social comparisons, not of actual necessities.

This aspect seemed to be in his mind when he tried to fortify his followers against the fear of persecution. "A disciple is not above his teacher, nor a servant above his lord. It is enough for the disciple that he be as his teacher, and the servant as his lord. If they have called the master of the house Beelzebub, how much more them of his household!" (Matthew 10. 24, 25.)

In saying those words to his disciples, Jesus was seeking to lift them from a timidity and caution begotten by their comparison with the secure and comfortable folk around them, to a fearlessness generated by a look at the greater persecution of their leader. This habit of looking up rather than around is a potent deliverer from fearfulness.

Here, again, however, Jesus' prescription of the upward look is more than a mere human effort. When men do look up to the birds of the heaven, they come to realize the Heavenly Father's continuing providential care. He feeds the tiny sparrows. He does not let one fall to the ground without his notice. His universe seems designed to support birds and flowers. "Fear not, therefore; ye are of more value than many sparrows" (Matthew 10. 31).

And when the disciples of Jesus look up from their human persecutors to their persecuted Leader, they find that behind the temporary shadow is the eventually victorious light. "Fear them not therefore: for there is nothing covered, that shall not be revealed; and hid, that shall not be known" (Matthew 10. 26). The universe has a divine publicity department. The inside facts work their way out. "Truth crushed to earth shall rise again." The righteous who today are down will have their reward, for

". . . behind the dim unknown
Standeth God within the shadow keeping watch
    above his own."

That is the confidence which delivers from the mood of defeatism and the fear of failure.

Moreover, Jesus, by a control of the forward look, would set his followers free from the fears which loom out of the future. Coming events have a way of casting shadows on some minds far out of proportion to their significance. For many years a Boston newspaper carried at the top of its editorial column these lines:

"Some of your hurts, you have cured,
    And the sharpest you still have survived;
But what torments of grief you've endured
    From the evils that never arrived!"

Jesus knew how much needless tribute men pay to the troubles that never arrive. Why, then, keep on borrowing trouble in advance? "Be not therefore anxious for the morrow: for the morrow will be anxious for itself. Sufficient unto the day is the evil thereof" (Matthew 6. 34). If men will let their worries wait until tomorrow, they will be surprised to find how many vanish like the mists of the morning. It is with our anxieties much as it is with a highway when we are motoring. When we are coming down the slope of one hill, the grade ahead may look forbiddingly steep, but when we start up that next hill, the grade seems to level itself out. Similarly, the tasks of tomorrow which look so frighteningly hard in advance have a way of straightening themselves out when we approach them in the fresh vigor of a new day. It was this very simple, practical principle which Jesus applied.

But with this forward look, as with the backward and upward focus, it was more than a matter of psychological method. Primarily it is the Heavenly Father's guarantee which banishes the fears of the future. Just as divine forgiveness, like the trainman's torch and signal, is our protection from the fears of the road behind, so faith in God is the searchlight which bores its way through the darkness to give the mind a clear track ahead.

And that searchlight of confident hope shines beyond the apparent terminus, death. Jesus is not reported as having said much about life beyond the grave. He took occasion to discuss the subject of immortality only with those like the Sadducees who doubted it, and with his disciples when they fell into moods of questioning it. At other times he seemed to take it for granted. "If it were not so, I would have told you" (John 14. 2). He so merged the kingdom of heaven with earthly experiences that the boundaries became blurred. The transition from the physical mansion in our "Father's House" to the "place prepared" is an incident of small concern when the heart has already followed its treasure into the realm where "neither moth nor rust doth consume, and where thieves do not break through nor steal" (Matthew 6. 20). The Heavenly Father is the guardian of the seen and the unseen. Such is the confidence which Jesus sought to impart to his disciples in order to dispel their fear of death. This future security should serve to steel men against the fears and pains of this present life. This was the protective armor which Jesus was trying to put on his persecuted disciples when he said, "Be not afraid of them which kill the body, but are not able to kill the soul" (Matthew 10. 28).

And then, after all this fortifying of his followers against fear—past, present, and future—Jesus says, "But I will warn you whom ye shall fear: Fear him, which after he hath killed hath power to cast into hell; yea, I say unto you, Fear him" (Luke 12. 5). The explanation of such a seemingly discordant note has divided the commentators. Some have held that Jesus could only be referring here to Satan, the enemy of souls. The majority, however, have come to hold that the one to be feared is God himself. To justify

this interpretation, they point out the difference
of construction in the two clauses. In relation
to those who "kill the body," the verbal construction indicates terror; in the second clause with
reference to "him who hath power to cast into
hell," the verbal form is that used elsewhere in a
higher and holier sense. (Note: The first clause
has $\mu\eta$ $\phi o\beta\eta\theta\tilde{\eta}\tau\epsilon$ $\dot{a}\pi\dot{o}$, the second has $\phi o\beta\dot{\eta}\theta\eta\tau\epsilon$.)
But accepting the majority opinion which holds
God and not Satan as the object of fear, what is
the "higher and holier" fear which Jesus enjoined
men to have toward a God whose Fatherly goodness he is stressing in the same context?

Jesus' picture of divine Fatherhood embodied
the elements of justice. His promises of divine
reward were based on confidence in that justice.
And justice carries a two-edged sword. "Take
heed that ye do not your righteousness before
men, to be seen of them: else ye have no reward
with your Father which is in heaven. When
therefore thou doest alms, sound not a trumpet
before thee, as the hypocrites do in the syna-
gogues and in the streets, that they may have
glory of men. Verily I say unto you, They have
received their reward" (Matthew 6. 1, 2). The
just Father in heaven takes account both of the
sincerely righteous and of the hypocritically pious.
Both are rewarded according to their spirit. But
in the case of the latter the implication is that

they have already received their reward in the empty glory of men. Henceforth, their fate is one of loss and futility.

This note of loss was the predominant color in Jesus' picture of the punishment meted out to the unrighteous. It was what they missed that made their hell. So it was in the picturesque parable of Dives. And the Gehenna of the "last judgment" passage is taken from the analogy of burning refuse. Damnation was wastage, salvation was salvage.

And what is more, this wastage which constituted hell was a result brought on the sinner by himself and not inflicted from outside by an avenging God. Jesus portrayed the unrighteous as cheating themselves out of the Kingdom. By not fulfilling the law they did not fulfill their lives. "Woe unto that man through whom the Son of man is betrayed!" (Matthew 26. 24.) If we apply that judgment to Judas, we might well ask who punished Judas for his betrayal? No outside agency or power was called in to condemn Judas. Judas punished himself. He took his own life. And if we lift the application from Judas to others who betray the cause of the Son of man, we see the general principle, as suggested by Jesus, that the punishment of sin comes not externally from God, but through ourselves. This is the truth which Francis Thompson rediscovered in the nineteenth century, when fleeing from his conscience he was ever hearing the Divine Voice calling over his shoulder, "All things betray thee who betrayest me."

Jesus gave no courtroom conception of God as a Judge imposing a law from outside ourselves. The force of divine justice, like the force of physical gravity, pervades the universe. By our adjustment to that force we determine our rewards and punishments. If we betray the Son of man, we find life betraying us. If, for instance, we abandon his basic principle of ministering rather than being ministered unto, ere long we begin to feel that life is not serving us with what we want. The home in which self-service rather than mutual ministering is the rule soon becomes a place in which the members feel cheated. The man who goes into a club or a community for what he can get out of it, rather than for what he can give to it, becomes, after a while, restless and disappointed. Thus the laws of the Kingdom as portrayed by Jesus work their way out. "There is nothing covered up, that shall not be revealed" (Luke 12. 2).

Such a conception of divine justice delivers a man from the fear of an avenging God whose motive is punishment, and from the fear of an arbitrary God whose punishments are mysterious. But there should remain a concern on man's part as

to what he may do to himself by failing to fulfill
the laws of divine justice. It is not unlike his
concern for the laws of gravity. Man lives and
moves and has his being in the grip of gravity,
but this does not cause the healthy person to go
around with a spirit of fearfulness. His consciousness of gravity gives him rather a sense of stability
and confidence. Jesus sought to free men from
the fear of an avenging justice and put them in
the grip of a sustaining justice. The sinner according to Jesus is not a convicted Jean Valjean,
hounded by an Inspector Javert, but, rather, a
shortsighted fool, cheating himself out of the
"kingdom prepared from the foundation of the
world."

The legitimate fear which remains for men in
the grip of a justly loving God is twofold. On
the one hand are the prudence and caution which
keep him from sinning away his own spiritual
sensitivity. Although unafraid of "them that kill
the body," man should be afraid of starving and
stifling his soul. The flaunting of divine love,
the resistance of good temptations, the repeated
evasions of responsibilities, the refusal to face
facts—these and their like leave the spirit in
progressive decay until, as in the case of Ibsen's
Peer Gynt, a man's nature deteriorates into life-
less layers of externals devoid of a vital core.
This peril remains after the picture of the venge-

ful God is removed.   And is that not what Jesus is suggesting in this same twelfth chapter of Luke when he speaks of the blasphemy against the Holy Spirit?   "And every one who shall speak a word against the Son of man, it shall be forgiven him: but unto him that blasphemeth against the Holy Spirit it shall not be forgiven" (Luke 12. 10).   The Heavenly Father holds no unforgiving vengeance against the enemies of the Son of man, but the person who through sin grows callous to the calls of the Holy Spirit, automatically shuts himself off from the chance of forgiveness.   The sons of God should fear the symptoms of soul decay.

The other legitimate phase of fear left to the followers of Jesus is that which is inspired by love itself.   "Perfect love casteth out fear, because fear hath punishment; and he that feareth is not made perfect in love" (1 John 4. 18).   True love banishes the fears which arise from self-interest and are flavored with the dread of punishment. But in freeing a man from the anxiety over what will happen to him, it places on him a concern as to what will happen to others.

The bad boy is afraid of his father because he dreads what the father will do to him; the good son is afraid that he will do something to hurt his father.   The coarse husband fears the penalties of his wife's anger; the fine nature is sensitive to

the pain of his wife's love.   Donald Hankey
looked at his "beloved captain" with fear, not a
dread of the punishment which that officer might
inflict on him, but of the sadness and disappointment which would be felt by the commander at
the disobedience or failure of his soldiers.

So Jesus tried to lift fear from the plane of
self-interest to the level of love.   Men are to fear
God as a good son is afraid to hurt his father, or
as a loving husband is afraid to mar his wife's happiness.   The cross was not a warning to impress
on men's minds the pain which will come to them
through sin; it was a symbol of the suffering which
comes to a Heavenly Father through the sins of
his children.

If the criticism is offered that this interpretation makes the fear of God too tame, and takes
the teeth out of the threat of hell, it might be said
that the person who is not restrained by this kind
of loving fear is already in the environs of hell.
He who is not responsive to God's love is hardened by that "blasphemy against the Holy Spirit"
which puts him beyond the pale of forgiveness
because it leaves him no longer repentant.   The
person who seeks salvation only through selfish
fear is still a coward.   Can a coward get into the
heaven of the courageous Jesus?   Would it be
heaven to him if he reached there?   Wherever
the spirit of selfish fear is, there is hell.

CHAPTER XV

THE LOVING ENEMIES

"MY mother, of whom I was very fond, recently passed away. Turning to the Bible for comfort, I ran across this passage: 'If any man cometh unto me, and hateth not his own father, and mother, and wife, and children, and brethren, and sisters, yea, and his own life also, he cannot be my disciple.' [Luke 14. 26.] How am I to understand such seemingly inhuman words coming from Jesus?"

This question from a radio listener, a bereaved daughter, expresses a puzzlement which has disconcerted and distressed uncounted readers. Hate is an emotion alien to the spirit of Jesus. Hatred of loved ones seems not only unchristian but unnatural.

The words which Luke reports of Jesus might be understandable on the lips of a medieval monk, who looked upon natural love as carnal and the family affections as a surrender to the flesh. But Jesus was no ascetic, no hater of "the good things of life." He did not go hurrying through this world as a vale of tears. He was no flagellant, finding virtue in self-torture and shunning human contacts. Although he suggested that it was not

201

expedient for some to marry, he limited the injunction by saying, "All men cannot receive this saying, but they to whom it is given" (Matthew 19. 11). Which persons were called to celibacy was apparently a matter of private judgment.

Jesus entered so vivaciously into human interests that he was a welcome guest at weddings (John 2. 1-11). He was interested in little children and drew them to him. As the eldest son in the carpenter's family at Nazareth, it may be assumed that he loyally helped to support his widowed mother. And according to the fourth Gospel, he was solicitous in the hour of his crucifixion for her future protection (John 19. 26, 27).

As a Jew, Jesus breathed the atmosphere of family loyalty, so beautifully characteristic of that race. Matthew records Jesus as reminding the scribes and Pharisees that "God said, Honor thy father and thy mother: and, He that speaketh evil of father or mother, let him die the death" (Matthew 15. 4). So ingrained was the family spirit in Jesus that he used the father-son relationship as the pattern by which to teach God's attitude toward man. "If ye then, being evil, know how to give good gifts unto your children, how much more shall your Father which is in heaven give good things to them that ask him?" (Matthew 7. 11.)

Not only did Jesus use family love as the pat-

tern of the divine-human relationship, but he
made brotherly love a prime requisite in man's
approach to God. A worshiper was to seek recon-
ciliation with his brother before he brought his
gifts to the altar of the Lord (compare Matthew
5. 23, 24). There was no validity in the emotional praise of a Heavenly Father which did not
eventuate in the practice of human fellowship.
The First Epistle of John reflects the teaching of
Jesus in its statement: "If a man say, I love God,
and hateth his brother, he is a liar: for he that
loveth not his brother whom he hath seen, cannot
love God whom he hath not seen" (1 John 4. 20).

Here, then, is the paradox: Jesus who forbade
men coming to the altar without first being reconciled to their fellows also forbade any person coming into his discipleship if "he hateth not his own
father, and mother, and wife, and children, and
brethren, and sisters, yea, and his own life also."
The apostle of love and unity calls for hatred and
separation. And this apparent contradiction is
not entirely dissolved by immersing it in the
milder parallel statement as given by Matthew:
"He that loveth father or mother more than me is
not worthy of me; and he that loveth son or
daughter more than me is not worthy of me"
(Matthew 10. 37). The difficulty remains that
this latter statement is accompanied by the idea of
schism and separation: "I came to set a man at

variance against his father, and the daughter against her mother, and the daughter-in-law against her mother-in-law: and a man's foes shall be they of his own household" (Matthew 10. 35, 36).

Jesus, who commanded his followers to love their enemies, warned them against their loving enemies.

In approaching this paradox of our friendly foes we face, first of all, Jesus' principle that the loves of the "natural man" need higher and holier loves to sustain them. We "fall in love" with certain other personalities. The expression suggests the spontaneity and naturalness of the process. The emotion may be kindled by the loveliness or lovableness of the other. Or the flame of affection may be stirred by the other's deeds of devotion. Or love may strike along a strange uncharted course like the flash of lightning from the heavens.

But these natural loves, so spontaneously ignited, lack the fuel to sustain themselves. They burn out. Within the marital bond, the emotion of love is not self-sustaining. It endures only when the lovers love and serve many things together and not merely each other. Husband and wife cannot preserve the rich flavor of affection by saying, "Go to, we shall devote ourselves exclusively to each other." When two persons set out with no interest higher than that of looking after each other, the relationship resembles the childish sport of teetering; when one is down the other is up, and each soon grows weary of watching the other's ups and downs. Comradeship, so essential to continuing love, requires a community of outside interests, a devotion to common causes.

Similarly, the parent-child relationship needs larger loyalties to preserve its wholesome balance. Left to itself, mother love, so incomparably beautiful, can so easily limit the child by the "silver spoon" which gives too much or by the "silver chord" which asks too much. Both parent and child should serve the whole self of the other, and that involves serving the need to serve. Many a youth is too long sheltered from the deep satisfaction which comes from meeting the need to be needed; and many a grandparent is too soon shelved away from the same satisfaction. Cruel as is the condition of the orphan thrown out on the world, almost as mutilating is the situation of the child shut in too much from the world. It was against this dwarfing paternalism that Jesus protested when he cried, "Suffer the little children to come unto me, and forbid them not." Life needs great commitments which catch it early and keep it late.

Friendship reveals the same requirement of

larger sustaining loves. Our finest personal com-
radeships are formed in circles of larger loyalties,
such as the love of a common Alma Mater or the
service of a common cause, even on the battlefield.
What happens to friendship when these supporting ties are removed may be seen at college class
reunions and American Legion conventions.
Two classmates share their campus activities until
they attain an attunement of spirit such that each
finds satisfaction in the presence and silent understanding of the other. They graduate and separate. Twenty years later they return for
commencement. They plan to renew their old
fellowship. They sit down together. But the old
sympathetic understanding does not flash between
them. They discuss business conditions, political
prospects, perhaps California climate and Florida
real estate. Their conversation ripples along in
the shallows but there is no deep which "calleth
unto deep." Their depth of friendship did not
long survive the cessation of common interests.

Thus our natural human affections need larger
and higher sustaining loves to save them from
inner dimming and shrinking. Therefore Jesus
did not leave love on the level of spontaneous
mutual reciprocity. "If ye love them that love
you, what reward have you?" (Matthew 5. 46.)
Jesus was realist enough to see the reward of that
kind of love in this present world. Even in our

most intimate circles love can deteriorate into a subtle form of selfishness. The possessive spirit so often tarnishes the marriage bond, making the home a counting house of rights and advantages rather than a co-operation of duties and devotions. Instead of being humbly grateful for the joy of giving to each other, husband and wife become irritated by the thought of what they are giving up for each other. The sensitive reverence for each other's personality disappears in this spirit of possessiveness. The ritual of affection is neglected.

Marriage ties are counted on to hold together persons who no longer exert themselves to hold the affection of the other, with the result that many think love can be preserved only by leaving it free from legal bonds. And, on the other hand, the inability to preserve the purity and stability of love without the marriage bond is evidenced by the human wreckage along our streets.

No, if your love is left to the mercy of "them that love you," if it has no deeper rootage than their reciprocal affection, it has no satisfying and enduring reward. Therefore, Jesus gave a deeper soil for the sustentation of human love. The love which Jesus enjoined grows out of the Heavenly Father's feeling for his children, "for he maketh his sun to rise on the evil and the good, and sendeth rain on the just and the unjust ' (Matthew 5. 45). The Divine Father's love is not limited by reciprocity treaties. It is free from the possessive spirit with its selfish calculations. And that is the quality of love which Jesus commanded the sons of the Father to feel toward their fellow men, friendly or hostile.

Jesus thus seemed to give his command to love with a kind of arbitrary military authority like that of a captain passing on an order from a higher command. Such an edict, standing alone, would be scarcely more emotionally effective than the command of a company lieutenant ordering his recruits to love their squad members. The response might very reasonably be similar to that of a certain sophisticated young woman who looked over a group of fellow church members and exclaimed, "God may love them, but I can't." Whereupon she left the company. Loving to order seems contrary to human nature.

But Jesus did not leave his command to love resting merely on the assertion of the Heavenly Father's unselfish love. Jesus gave a formula whereby human nature can generate this godlike quality of love toward the unlovely and the un- lovable. He said, "Do good to them that hate you, bless them that curse you, and pray for them that despitefully use you" (Luke 6. 27, 28; com- pare Matthew 5. 44). By such aggressive good

will a person begets love.   In his enemies?   Perhaps, although not necessarily.   But primarily in
himself.   Love in an individual, according to
Jesus' teaching, is generated basically not by what
others do to him, which is the publicans' way of
reckoning, but by what he does to others.   By
blessing, praying, and doing good men can love
to order.

The truth in this paradoxical principle may be
seen embedded in certain homely maxims and
experiences.   It is a common saying that if you
wish to make a friend, get him to do something
for you, whereas, if you wish to lose a friend, get
him in debt to yourself.   The cynical would say
that this is evidence of human ingratitude.   Perhaps so.   But is it not more significantly the proof
of the gospel principle that the sons of men, like
the Son of man, come not to be ministered unto
but to minister?   Personalities are held perma-
nently together by the services which they render
to each other rather than by the gifts which they
receive from each other.   This is due to the fact
that the deepest hunger of the human spirit is the
need to be needed.   On that psychological basis
rests Jesus' paradox of the lifting yoke and also
his seemingly contradictory formula of cost-regu-
lated love.

Something in human nature makes a mother's
heart go out with an added load of tenderness

toward the little ugly duckling or the recklessly wayward son. Something there is which causes a true father to feel a special nearness to the child which needs him most. Was not this what Jesus had in mind when he asked, "What man of you, having a hundred sheep, and having lost one of them, doth not leave the ninety and nine in the wilderness, and go after that which is lost, until he find it? And when he hath found it, he layeth it on his shoulders, rejoicing. And when he cometh home, he calleth together his friends and his neighbors, saying unto them, Rejoice with me, for I have found my sheep which was lost" (Luke 15. 3-6). That special joy over the recovery of the wanderer which cost so much searching and heartache—that is human nature. And said Jesus, that is also the divine nature. "I say unto you, that even so there shall be joy in heaven over one sinner that repenteth, more than over ninety and nine righteous persons, which need no repentance" (Luke 15. 7).

This statement does not mean that God is more concerned to save one soul than another. The God who "maketh his sun to rise on the evil and the good" is "no respecter of persons." But it does mean that a father's love, even a Heavenly Father's, gains glow in proportion to the effort expended. Our loves, like our possessions, appreciate in value according to their cost. Where the treasure is, there is the heart also. The love which Jesus commanded is insured by the payment of premiums, not by the receipt of dividends.

This quality of love is purged of its possessive self-interestedness. It is fortified against the gusty fluctuations of mood. Since it is not merely the reflection of the environing lovableness and kindness but the incandescence of one's own surcharged spirit, such love is able to keep burning in the coldest and darkest surroundings. By this godlike self-generating love, Jesus safeguarded the natural affections from their own inner decay.

He also sought to deliver human love from its softening protectiveness as well as from its vitiating possessiveness. Jesus reveled in the re-enforcing friendship of his disciples. Those twelve were not only his instruments for perpetuating his program; they were also the means of preserving the fullness and radiance of his own spirit. A solitary Son of man would have come far short of Jesus of Nazareth. In fact, no solitary Saviour could reach and redeem the sons of men. Yet with all his reliance on the friendship of his disciples, Jesus knew the dangers which arise from love's desire to protect. When the devoted Peter sought to restrain his Master from risking his life in Jerusalem, Jesus uttered the stinging words, "Get thee behind me, Satan: for thou mindest not the

things of God, but the things of men" (Mark 8.
33).

And did not Jesus have to resist this same protective passion within his own family? The
record reveals that the Nazarene friends understood not his program, thinking that he was "beside himself." No doubt his family tried more
than once to dissuade him from his dangerous
course. This must have been their mission on
that occasion which called forth the enigmatic
utterance of Jesus, "Who is my mother?" "And
there come his mother and brethren; and, standing without, they sent unto him, calling him.
And a multitude was sitting about him; and they
say unto him, Behold, thy mother and thy
brethren without seek for thee. And he an-
swereth them, and saith, Who is my mother and
my brethren? And looking around on them
which sat round about him, he saith, Behold, my
mother and my brethren! For whosoever shall
do the will of God, the same is my brother, and
sister, and mother" (Mark 3. 31-35).

Here apparently Jesus was experiencing in his
own family that which has so frequently hindered
the kingdom of God. Love, in its desire to shelter its own, holds them back from that exposure
which toughens moral fiber and from that abandon which advances the frontiers of social progress. Not every public servant has had the kind

of helpmeet that Wendell Phillips found in his wife, who was accustomed to take his hand before he went out to face his hostile audiences and to bid him Godspeed with the words, "Don't shilly-shally, Wendell." Sinclair Lewis, in his new book, *It Can't Happen Here,* plays up the weakening and taming effect of the thought, "But I have a wife and family to support." The bonds of love may so easily become the barriers to men's larger loyalties. In this sense, "a man's foes shall be they of his own household."

It was to prevent the protective and possessive elements of love from crippling men's great commitments that Jesus said, "He that loveth father or mother more than me is not worthy of me" (Matthew 10. 37). It was the same truth which Luke put in the negative with cutting sharpness, "If any man cometh unto me, and hateth not his own father, and mother, . . . he cannot be my disciple" (Luke 14. 26). A sharp saying? Yes. But it is the kindly sharpness of healing surgery. When lesser loyalties slip out of place and thereby hinder larger loyalties, they must be reset, though it be painful at the time. And, in the long run, conscientious and intelligent loyalty to Jesus never leaves personal love impoverished or mutilated.

Perhaps a word of explanation should be given to the reported term, "hateth." The occasion for hate may arise within the circles of love, as it did in the case of Peter's effort to restrain his Master from going to Jerusalem. The lightning flash of Jesus' righteous indignation struck not at Peter, the man, but at his Satanic suggestion. Jesus could hate sin and yet love the sinner, whereas human beings tend to hate the sinner and love the sin. Jesus' anger flashed out in the Temple when he saw the money-changers transforming it from a house of prayer into a den of thieves; but it was the sin, not the sinners, at which his anger was aimed. Even when the nails were piercing his hands, there was no personal hatred. "Father, forgive them; for they know not what they do" (Luke 23. 34). Hatred, as Jesus manifested it, is the lightning flash which clears the air but does not strike the person.

Yet we must not allow the lightning flashes of righteous hatred to blind us to the basic emphasis of Jesus' teaching. In his program hatred was to love in the proportion and relation of lightning to sunshine. When lesser interests and loyalties roll up to becloud the horizon and separate the spirit from God, then the electric flash may come, but the abiding light is from the sun behind the cloud. In the realm of love there must be a central and sustaining sun. In the kingdom of God, as in the governments of men, there must be a sovereign power. According to Jesus, that central sun and sovereign power is the love of God, which he claimed to represent and reveal.

In that light shall man see light (compare Psalm 36. 9). By its attraction, man's other loves are held in their proper orbits. By adjusting his position to that divine source of light man may be sure that his shadow of influence falls with beneficent effect on his other circles of love. The merely conscientious person may go about watching his shadow and wondering how each deed will affect those around him, thereby spoiling his virtues with priggishness and his influence with self-consciousness. But the follower of Jesus is not always eying the effects of his conduct, nor is he afraid of his shadow. He seeks to "get right" with God as revealed in Jesus, believing that true fidelity to the way of Jesus never makes one a disloyal son, an inconsiderate husband, or a cruel father, whatever may be the feeling about him at the moment.

CHAPTER XVI

THE PEACEFUL SWORD

SOME time ago a high officer of the United States Army was credited with a neat explanation of Jesus' attitude toward the use of physical force. He admitted that in the early popular period of his ministry the Master had said, "Love your enemies." But after longer experience with the perversity of men, Jesus changed his mind, and said, "Think not that I came to send peace on the earth: I came not to send peace, but a sword" (Matthew 10. 34). The General's reasoning sounds plausible. Up in the sunny Galilean days, amid the successes of his early healing work, it was easy to preach love even to enemies; but as the opposition hardened, it would have been natural for Jesus to renounce peaceful proposals and to advocate resort to arms.

Such a change of attitude on Jesus' part would have been quite in line with the way of the world. The students of one nation fraternize with the students of other lands in the comradeship of the campus and then go forth to kill them as alumni. When Harvard University dedicated her memorial church to those sons who died in the Great War, the question arose as to whether the roll of honor should include the names of those who died on the German side as well as those who fell with the Allies. A "natural" question, but was it a "natural" situation? Diplomats drink their toasts of friendship to the representatives of other countries today, and tomorrow march forth to kill them, or to be more accurate, summon their fellow men to go out and slay them.

But to ascribe a similar militarization of mind to Jesus hardly tallies with the total impression given by the Gospels. It is true that at first glance a passage in Luke seems to give support to the General's thesis: "And he said unto them, When I sent you forth without purse, and wallet, and shoes, lacked ye anything? And they said, Nothing. And he said unto them, But now, he that hath a purse, let him take it, and likewise a wallet; and he that hath none, let him sell his cloak and buy a sword. For I say unto you, that this which is written must be fulfilled in me, And he was reckoned with the transgressors: for that which concerneth me hath fulfillment. And they said, Lord, behold, here are two swords. And he said unto them, It is enough" (Luke 22. 35-38).

It would be absurd, however, to take such words literally as advocating the adoption of the sword for defense. Jesus was far too shrewd to think that two swords would be enough to ward off the attacks of the hostile host. There must have been a parabolic significance in his reference to the swords.

Furthermore, Jesus is recorded as having commanded Peter to put up his sword when the arrest did take place. "Put up again thy sword into its place: for all they that take the sword shall perish with the sword" (Matthew 26. 52). This renunciation of physical force in the garden at the end of his earthly ministry was consistent with his refusal of such material means in the wilderness temptation at the beginning of his public career. From his temptation to his trial Jesus held to his principle of nonviolence.

His refusal of the sword, however, did not mean passivity. To be smitten on one cheek and then to do nothing might be misunderstood as cowardice or weakness; but to "turn the other cheek" (compare Matthew 5. 39) would at least strike the curiosity of the assailant. To carry the equipment of a domineering Roman soldier the one mile which was compulsory might be taken as mere sullen surrender to necessity; but to carry the burden "a second mile" would arrest the attention and arouse the interest. If a litigant sued you at law and took away your coat without any resistance on your part, he would probably assume the weakness of your case, but if you gave him "your cloak also" the act would certainly set him thinking.

Pacifism, as Jesus taught it, was active good will,
not inert nonresistance.   Inertia does not make
for brotherhood but against it.   Left to themselves
our circles of brotherly feeling contract rather
than expand, not only from inner possessiveness
and protectiveness but also from outer rebuffs and
disappointments.   After contact with a few cold
shoulders the tendency is to try fewer locked arms.

". . . the whips and scorns of time,
The oppressor's wrong, the proud man's con-
    tumely,
The pangs of despised love, the law's delay,
The insolence of office and the spurns
That patient merit of the unworthy takes"

—these constitute "a sea of troubles" from which
sensitive souls withdraw into the heart-locked
harbors of self-centeredness and self-defense.
When Jesus commanded love to follow the line
of nonresistance, he was not telling it to follow
the line of least resistance.

When love stands still, it loses ground.   Fellowship is a realm in which one has to keep working forward to stay where he is.   Jesus realized
the struggle required to resist the encroaching
restrictions of distrust and dislike, of provincialism and prejudice.

And if the boundaries of brotherhood were to
be extended, still more effort was necessary.   To

expand the family pattern so that "whosoever shall do the will of God, the same is my brother, and sister, and mother" (Mark 3. 35) is a stretching toward perfection which seems impossible to the "natural man." The Gospels appear to have distinguished between the intimate affection which one feels for his own family and the "love" to outsiders. After the hazards of reporting and translation, it is hard to know how much weight should be given to the fact that in speaking of love within the family circle, the Gospels use the word φιλέω, whereas in commanding love to neighbors and enemies the Greek verb ἀγαπάω is employed. Nevertheless, it does seem significantly suggestive of Jesus' realism that he should be interpreted as using in home relationships the affectionate word and in outside contacts a term implying active good will.

But active good will, this latter form of love, is an attainment requiring strenuous cultivation. Jesus experienced the difficulty of breaking through the provincialism and traditionalism of a guileless Nathanael in order to make him see that a "good thing" could "come out of Nazareth." In his effort to lengthen a certain lawyer's radius of neighborliness, Jesus told the parable of the Good Samaritan, but even that unforgettable story apparently failed to bring the scribe into the kingdom-of-God range of neighborhood. And lest

the judgment of posterity rest too hard on the
Jewish lawyer, it should be remembered that when
a certain Samaritan village refused to accord Jesus
hospitality, his own disciples, James and John,
wanted to call down fire from heaven and consume the place (see Luke 9. 51-55). To pray for
them that persecute you, to have active good will
toward enemies was a perfection of love seen once
on the cross but approximated by comparatively
few followers of the cross. To extend the con-
cept of neighbor to foreigners is an attainment
which after nineteen centuries men have achieved
very imperfectly, for our own United States feels
called upon to spend over a billion dollars a year
for armament in order to prove its "good-neigh-
bor" policy.

The difficulties encountered in extending the
boundaries of brotherhood cast a deepening
shadow on Jesus' mind as his work went on. He
saw how the moods of brotherliness fluctuated
even in his own chosen company. He observed
how appeals for voluntary kindness and charity
fell short of securing justice, the possessors of
privilege being unwilling to yield any more than
they were forced to do. He realized how easily
charity becomes tainted with condescension and
pride, "the leaven of the Pharisees." He noted
that mere contact with others did not beget
brotherhood, but, rather, the closer men came to-

gether physically often the farther apart they grew
socially, for physical nearness frequently made
people more conscious of their differences. Jerusalem, where men were massed together, had
sharper social and racial tensions than the rural
regions. The city "melting pot" was the cauldron
of explosives—a fact quite as impressive in the
twentieth century as in the first. Jesus was aware
too that so many would-be righteous persons were
not using their imaginations sufficiently to make
their goodness brotherly. They thought they
were practicing his Golden Rule, but they had
not taken the pains to picture what they would
wish done to themselves if they were in the others'
places. If charged with neglecting the law of
love, they would have been surprised, saying,
"Lord, when saw we thee hungry, or athirst, or a
stranger, or naked, or sick, or in prison, and did
not minister unto thee?"   (Matthew 25. 44.)
Their love was blind—not to the defects but to
the needs of others.

After all Jesus' preaching of love to man and
love to God, men still failed to see the inseparabil-
ity of the two or to feel the range and force of
either. More and more he became convinced that
drastic efforts must be taken if a brotherly society
was to be developed. The banishment of open
strife could be accomplished by nothing less than
an inner warfare against the spiritual foes of

inertia, indifference, distrust, prejudice, and their like. It was this conviction which caused him to exclaim, "Think not that I came to send peace on the earth; I came not to send peace, but a sword" (Matthew 10. 34). He used the military symbol to sharpen the assertion that the fight for fellowship requires as insistent and sacrificial effort as men manifest on the field of battle. Jesus of Nazareth was a fighter for fellowship.

Both fighting and fellowship represent something basic in human nature. This fact is revealed in the common sayings, "Men like a fighter" and "All the world loves a lover." The Son of man manifested both. But the point at which we have so tragically departed from Jesus in this regard is that he fought *for* fellowship while we fight *against* it. Jesus attacked the evil without ceasing to love the evildoer. In our intimate family circles we sometimes approximate such an attitude. "What son is there whom his father chasteneth not?" And the motive of parental chastening is ostensibly that of love. Yet so prone is personal resentment to creep even into parental love that when a punishing father says, "This hurts me worse than it does you," his statement does not always carry conviction—at least to the recipient of the painful corrective.

And in circles outside the family we fight the evildoer and preserve the evil. In war we hate

the enemy and copy their methods. We killed
the Huns and kept the war system.

Our human attitudes are still at the low level
where righteous indignation is not aroused without personal hatred. During the Great War we
in America were stirred to fever heat of anger by
the sight of enemies in human form. But after
the flesh-and-blood enemy was removed and only
the war system remained, that impersonal foe no
longer fired our zeal. When, a dozen or more
years after the armistice, a President declared,
"We must wage peace as men have waged war,"
his challenge failed to stir any depth of public
interest.

Our practice has fallen from the apostolic plane
where it could be said, "Our wrestling is not
against flesh and blood, but against the principali-
ties, against the powers, against the world-rulers
of this darkness, against the spiritual hosts of
wickedness in the heavenly places" (Ephesians 6.
12).

Jesus came with his sword to lead the fight for
fellowship by lifting the struggle from that against
"flesh and blood" to that against "the spiritual
hosts of wickedness." He would displace the
smoldering personal hatreds which leave their
poisons in both the hater and the hated and re-
place them with a righteous indignation which
cleanses like a refiner's fire. He would have his

followers wage peace as aggressively as men have
hitherto waged war, for the activity of good spirits
is the only safeguard against the return of the evil
spirits (Matthew 12. 43-45). If men are to overcome evil with good, they must make that good as
colorful in content, as arresting in appeal and as
stirring in challenge as is the evil to be con-
quered.

This is a point at which the followers of Jesus
have failed in their desire to supplant war with
peace. They have allowed the warmakers to
monopolize the great colorful stirring concepts,
such as patriotism and heroism. When the public
thinks of patriots, it thinks of those who answer
the call to arms. Patriotic societies are those
which perpetuate the memories of past military
victories or prepare for future ones. When the
man on the street is asked to name a nation's
heroes, he almost invariably begins with those in
uniform. Militarism connotes bravery, red-
blooded strength. Pacifism is negative, anaemic.
Christendom has not yet caught the dynamic creative quality which was in Jesus' peacemaking program.

But how far is it legitimate to project Jesus'
principle of the sword into the complex situations of peacemaking? He himself did not extend
his principle with explicit applications beyond
local boundaries. His refusal to lead a revolution

against Rome showed his reliance on spiritual rather than physical force in social reform. His reported utterance on the occasion of his arrest, "They that take the sword shall perish with the sword," indicated his insight into the utter futility of war. But in connection with the tribute money his injunction to "render therefore unto Caesar the things that are Caesar's" (Matthew 22. 21) implies his recognition of the State's right to coerce.

How far, then, can the element of coercion enter into the fight for fellowship? In fidelity to Jesus' principle of nonresistance must his followers submit to coercion when the power behind it is unjust? Or what is more difficult to answer, can Christians resort to coercion in order to correct injustice which voluntary appeals fail to remove? On these points the thinking of the Church is very confused. The refrain of the liberal social gospel has been that voluntary co-operation is superior to coercion and hence must and will prevail. But the middle-class churches which deprecate the use of coercion or violence in effecting social change are still predominantly advocates of force and preparedness in international contacts. And, on the other hand, many left-wing liberals who avow an absolutist pacifist position in disputes between nations have become convinced that social justice at home cannot be secured by appealing to the voluntary kindness of the privileged classes.

With this confusion of situation in mind, Reinhold Niebuhr writes: "The Christian who lives in, and benefits from, a society in which coercive economic and political relationships are taken for granted, all of which are contrary to the love absolutism of the gospels, cannot arbitrarily introduce the uncompromising ethics of the gospel into one particular issue."[1] To be sure, contemporary living has become such a muddied stream of mingled compromises that it cannot be cleansed by the infusion of the perfectly ideal position on a single issue any more than the turgid current of the lower Hudson can be purified by pouring into it a tank of crystal spring water from its Adirondack source. The person who takes the absolutist pacifist position in all relationships is in danger of ignoring or sacrificing human values at some points. His nonresisting love with its appeal to voluntary kindness may leave a truculent Italy to wreak injustice on little Ethiopia or a greedy coal operator to deprive the miner of life, liberty, and the pursuit of happiness.

The only adequate corrective for our commingled compromises and confused thinking would be a social planning which could put into

[1] Reinhold Niebuhr, *An Interpretation of Christian Ethics*, p. 186. Harper & Brothers, New York.

operation the original formula: "Thou shalt love thy neighbor as thyself." But inasmuch as the slightest efforts at social planning raise the cry of regimentation and arouse intense opposition, it seems an elusive goal to propose the possibility of a new birth for nations or societies. As a gospel for groups, the preaching of the cross is still "unto Jews a stumbling block, and unto Gentiles foolishness." Hence the individual with his ideals must continue to function in the midst of systems composed of cruel compromises. This fact helps to constitute the sword which Jesus brought to his followers, a sword which symbolizes not only the intensity of their fight for fellowship but also the suffering inflicted on themselves by the conflict of loyalties.

Hearing the cries for justice and seeing the deafness of the unjust, the follower of Jesus must decide whether voluntary appeals to the goodness of men may have to be supplemented by coercive resistance to the badness of men. In reaching that decision he has for his guidance no map of our complex social situation, but he does have some signposts left by Jesus. The basic test of social action is reverence for personality. Do violent methods of correction improve or damage these personal values? The testimony of experience seems to register an emphatic "No." If certain wars and revolutions seem to have advanced human rights, the question still remains whether the ends might not have been achieved by better ways. When injustices have been cleared away by violence, the seeds of further evils have been sown. The prophetic prediction of "beating the swords into plowshares" never went so far as to promise that swords would serve as plowshares. The fruits of the Spirit—joy, love, peace, and their like—do not grow on landscape tilled with the sword.

When the issue comes to a clear-cut choice, it would seem that the follower of Jesus must choose to be persecuted rather than to kill. The point of the Christian's conscientious objection is not his refusal to give life but his refusal to take life. It is the way of the cross as against the way of the sword.

But coercion which comes short of killing is another question. Jesus did not denounce the existence of courts and prisons although he counseled men to settle their disputes without resort to litigation (Matthew 5. 25). He had friendly contacts with Roman centurions (Matthew 8. 5-13), and is not reported as having inveighed against the presence of the police. These instruments of government Jesus appeared to take for granted as a part of the state's legitimate function. Coercion, therefore, exercised for the preservation of human rights, administered in an impartial, not a vengeful spirit, is quite consonant with the teaching of Jesus. There can be a Christian police power, local and international. There cannot be a Christian war system.

The fight for fellowship is not to be won by a mere formula so simple as that of the absolutist pacifist position. It requires commitments quite as costly and much more complex. It calls for conscientious objectors to war, certainly, but also for constructive creators of peace. It summons men to mobilize their resources, mental and material, for the eradication of the causes of strife and for the cultivation of the means of co-operation. There is a war to end war—not the eye-for-eye kind seen in Europe twenty years ago, but the love-for-hate kind seen in Palestine nineteen centuries ago.

And while it seems a futile dream to project the gospel of the cross from individuals to groups and nations, it should be remembered that there is a God of the "salt" and the "light" and the "leaven" to whose power thoughtful men cease to set limits. Sir Josiah Stamp in his recent presidential address before the British Association for the Advancement of Science challenged the belief that each generation will live much like that which preceded. Sir Josiah agrees with Whitehead: "We are living in the first period of human history for which this assumption is false." It may be unwarranted modern pride that declares ours to be the first period in which the vicious circles of recurring evils can be broken and society can be remade to order. But certainly the acceleration of change has shattered the static view of human nature. No longer is it intelligent to declare that war, as the world knows it, is inevitable because "man is a fighting animal, always has been, and always will be." Man's militancy can be redirected to fight for fellowship rather than against it. Even governments can learn the use of the peaceful sword.

CHAPTER XVII

THE WINNING LOSERS

FIRMLY embedded in the mind of our race is the old maxim, "Self-preservation is nature's first law." When a person is driven down to the rock-bottom decisions between life and death, the popular assumption is that he will struggle to the last ditch in order to save himself. Unselfish sentiments and noble ideals may move over his mind as the patches of light and shadow chase one another across an autumnal landscape, but, as Theodore Dreiser essayed to show in *An American Tragedy,* when life corners a man, he will sacrifice everything to save himself. That is the realistic principle on which our political economy and our social philosophy are based.

Was Jesus, then, trying to reverse the main drive of human motivation when he said, not once, but repeatedly according to the record, "Whosoever would save his life shall lose it; but whosoever shall lose his life for my sake, the same shall save it" (Luke 9. 24; compare Luke 17. 33; Matthew 10. 39; Matthew 16. 25)? Was he a Canute in futile fashion trying to sweep back the ocean of self-interest with his command of self-sacrifice? Is this paradoxical principle of saving life by losing it just a pathetic reminder of the huge joke which self-seeking society has played upon the idealists and martyrs?

Of course there are some rather easy ways of explaining this seemingly impractical paradox. For one thing, it may be said that this gospel pronouncement was meant for the times of the martyrs. The person who lost his life for the sake of Jesus' new movement would be guaranteed entrance into the life eternal. The context reveals this as the immediate implication. Undoubtedly many a Christian martyr died, thinking he was effecting a clear-cut and sure exchange of his earthly physical life for an immortal existence in heaven. If a person may choose between losing a few years of security on earth and gaining eternal safety in heaven, the devout believer will be inclined to balance the scales on the side of the latter. An evangelist's illustration remains engraved on the mind of the writer since childhood. "If," said the evangelist, "a bird were to visit this earth once in a million years, and were to carry away a grain of sand at each trip, when it carried away the entire earth, eternity would only have begun." Such a vivid picture of eternal length would make any temporary sacrifice on this earth seem a good bargain.

But Jesus did not seem to draw such clear-cut

distinctions between the life here and the life hereafter. The gospel uses the same word for the "life" which men were bidden to "lose" as for the "life" which they were promised to "save." This specific statement does not warrant the interpretation that men are to give up physical existence for the winning of immortal life. And neither does the general program of Jesus. He came to give life, and give it abundantly here and now. He was born among people who were being crushed and cramped by hard conditions. He knew that his countrymen desired to save themselves from these oppressive circumstances and to secure a larger life. His announced purpose in the first recorded synagogue appearance at Nazareth was to fulfill the prophetic promises of Isaiah in giving release to the captives, sight to the blind, liberty to the bruised, and good tidings to the poor. Jesus began his work partly as a physician, healing the bodies, feeding the hungry, comforting the sorrowful. Granted that this redemptive work was on a scale so large that its horizons embraced a kingdom of heaven unseen and eternal as well as visible and temporal, nevertheless Jesus did not work on the principle of bartering earthly suffering for future paradise. Hence we can hardly explain the paradox by the interpretation that we are to lose the present existence for the sake of winning a future spiritual safety.

A second explanation might be offered to soften this hard saying. Perhaps this choice between losing and saving was intended only for the heroic emergencies of life. While self-preservation is nature's first law, it is also a fact of experience that a true mother will give her life for her child, a devoted husband will die for his wife, a loyal officer will perish at his post to save his ship. These bursts of luminous loyalty lighten the darkness and reveal something deep in human nature which does count certain things dearer than life itself. Jesus, therefore, may have been calling for cross-bearers to stab the world's darkness with some lightning flashes of this heroic love.

Such demonstrations do have their value. A picket frozen on duty, a mother starved for her brood, a Stephen stoned for his faith, a Cavell shot for her humanitarianism and saying "Patriotism is not enough"—these do open the eyes of men to something more glorious than self-preservation. But such examples of self-sacrifice are related to the general activities of life as the geysers of Yellowstone Park are to the force of gravity. "Old Faithful" shoots its stream of water upward, but that does not alter the fact that the prevailing trend of rainfall and waterfall is downward. Were the cross of Jesus and the crosses to which he called his disciples intended to be merely spec-

tacular geysers showing to what heights love can
lift itself when under deep pressure?

We believe not. If Jesus had looked upon his
principle of sacrifice as an heroic outburst of love
in life's emergencies, he would not have talked
about it. The Master who knew human nature
so perfectly realized the note of unreality in any
one who goes about asserting his willingness to die
for others. The husband, for instance, who repeatedly tells his wife that he would gladly die for
her is quite often one who does not live or work
very sacrificially for her. And the patrioteer who
shouts his determination to give his life for his
beloved land is frequently one who so profiteers
on his country that others almost wish he *would*
go out and die for it. We suspect the sincerity of
those who parade their sacrificial purposes.
When we see the apparel of heroism on parade,
we call it "heroics."

Jesus was against all "heroics." When Peter
waxed emotional and exclaimed, "If all shall be
offended in thee, I will never be offended" (Matthew 26. 33). "Even if I must die with thee, yet
will I not deny thee" (Matthew 26. 34, 35),
Jesus deflated the pretentious devotion with the
sharp rejoinder: "Verily I say unto thee, that this
night, before the cock crow, thou shalt deny me
thrice" (Matthew 26. 34). No, Jesus did not desire his disciples to swear that they would be brave

in time of emergency. With his gentlemanly re-
serve, he knew that such heroic sacrifices come as
the silent spontaneous outcropping of deep life
currents.

When Jesus declared, "Whosoever would save
his life shall lose it; but whosoever shall lose his
life for my sake, the same shall save it," he was
not talking merely about religious martyrdoms
and heroic emergencies. He was laying down a
deep principle of which these are but occasional
dramatic eruptions.

Jesus took it for granted that men desire to
save themselves. He based his appeal on that
assumption. "For what shall a man be profited,
if he shall gain the whole world, and forfeit his
life? or what shall a man give in exchange for his
life?" (Matthew 16. 26.) It was on this realistic
recognition of self-preservation as nature's first
law that Jesus proceeded to assert his paradox of
saving by losing.

A. *Who Find by Losing*

One phase of this paradoxical principle is that
men find their lives by losing sight of them. "He
that findeth his life shall lose it; and he that loseth
his life for my sake shall find it" (Matthew 10.
39). Jesus reversed the popular prescription for
self-preservation which is to look out for Number
One.

The psychological validity of the Nazarene contention begins to appear on second thought. The
initial trouble with the fellow who is always looking out for Number One is that he thereby fails
to see the real and whole Number One. A man
can see certain superficial features of himself by
studying himself in a mirror, but photographers
do not get the best results by taking pictures of
persons while they are looking in mirrors. The
most revealing photographs are those taken of un-
studied expressions when the subject's mind is
diverted to something outside himself. Similarly,
while most persons should spend more time in
studying themselves, nevertheless self-study is not
the highest and most effective way to self-dis-
covery. Meditation may become too introspec-
tive and lead to introversion. Like the music of
a happily short-lived popular song, thoughts may
"go round and round" and come out nowhere.
Hence as a mode of finding the real self, meditation must be supplemented, and at times super-
seded, by adoration.

Thus Jesus showed a truer insight than did
the Greeks. He did not assert as the first law of
learning, "Know Thyself." To Jesus, as to his
Hebrew predecessors, the first and great commandment was, "Thou shalt love the Lord thy
God with all thy heart, and with all thy soul, and
with all thy mind" (Matthew 22. 37; compare

Deuteronomy 6. 5). Not by microscopic introspection do we piece together the puzzle picture
of personality, but by losing sight of ourselves in
telescopic adoration of the God who made heaven
and earth. Jesus used the same psychological
principle in the prayer which he taught his disciples. The Lord's Prayer begins not with an
inward look at our hungers for daily bread or at
our trespasses, but with a mind-stretching contemplation of "Our Father who art in heaven"
and of His kingdom which is coming (Matthew
6. 9, 10).

This losing sight of self aids in the discovery of
self not only because it breaks the vicious and
blinding circle of introversion but also because it
reveals those deeper needs which mere meditation leaves hidden. It is the stretching of the
mind as of the muscle which makes aware of its
limitations. The need of growth is one which we
do not discover symmetrically and satisfactorily
by looking at ourselves or by comparison with
human beings around us. Introspection is often
too static or one-sided; comparisons with others
are often too confusing. "They themselves, measuring themselves by themselves, and comparing
themselves with themselves, are without understanding" (2 Corinthians 10. 12). These street-
level studies and comparisons tend toward a clubbable atmosphere of mutual exoneration, or

toward Pharisaical pride or toward personal despair. From this welter our view of ourselves is saved by the lift of a long horizon, the adoration of an Ideal One in whose presence and purposes we lose ourselves.

Moreover, this losing of self reveals not only hidden needs but also otherwise undiscovered powers. A faithful daughter gives herself to a stricken mother through long months of illness. When the long fight is over and the crisis is passed, she looks back at her effort and exclaims, "I did not know it was in me to go through all that." She had manifested an energy and endurance which she could not calculate in advance nor summon at will. She had tapped hitherto unknown and unused reservoirs of strength. By losing sight of herself in looking after her mother she had joined forces with "him that is able to do exceeding abundantly above all that we ask or think, according to the power that worketh in us" (Ephesians 3. 20).

The paradox of self-knowledge is that we must enter through the exits. It is a platitude to say that the person who is always hunting for happiness does not find it. That was the error of Epicureanism. It is not quite so trite but equally true, that the individual who keeps consciously cultivating his own virtues tends to harden them into juiceless self-righteousness. That was the

fallacy of Stoic philosophy.   Jesus avoided both
with his principle of self-finding through self-forgetting.

Almost a century ago Emerson entered in his
Journal the following sentence: "Henry Thoreau
made last night the fine remark that as long as a
man stands in his own way, everything seems to
be in his way—government, society, and even the
sun, moon and stars, as astrology may testify"
(*Journal*, October, 1842).   Thus the principle of
looking out for Number One defeats itself.   A
man gets in his own way, thereby blurring his
vision of himself and of his world.   "He that findeth his life shall lose it; and he that loseth his life
for my sake shall find it."

B.   *Who Save by Spending*

A second principle involved in Jesus' prescription for self-preservation is that we save ourselves
by spending ourselves.   We cannot hoard life as
we can money.   When a person tries to be a
miser of his own health, he usually makes himself
miserable.   The persons who are ever talking
about conserving their strength, who are con-
stantly watching for symptoms and coddling their
complaints—such individuals become slaves to the
thermometer and fugitives from germs, living
below par and dying before their time.   We develop our own physical strength by expending it,

and that exercise is most beneficial which takes our mind off the need of doing it.

Similarly, we enlarge our mental powers by spending them to the limit and thereby extending their limits. The intelligent student does not say, "Since I shall need all my mental strength in my lifework after I leave college, I shall conserve it during these four years." Some students, it must be admitted, do seem to act on that principle, but it does not work. Mental talents, like those of the parable, are not to be buried in a napkin, but put to use, thereby gaining an increment and fitting their possessor for larger endeavors. Whosoever would save his memory shall lose it. The proper educational process is not a cistern method of collecting the ideas which drip off the eaves of the professors' minds, but rather is it a tapping of the artesian springs of intellectual interest. And springs are saved by keeping the outward-bound channel open.

Our emotional nature reveals the fallacy of saving by conserving even more clearly. In a recent book one of the characters, a sheltered woman, asked that she not be made to sympathize with people any more often than necessary, for sympathy put such an exhausting strain on her emotions. Such a conservation policy dries up the milk of human kindness. A mother's love is not diluted by having to be divided among a dozen children. But the cautious person, who is afraid to give himself very far to others lest he be taken in by them, will find the boundaries of his affection shrinking. Love, sympathy, appreciation do not exhaust themselves by use. They are saved by being spent.

A talented literary woman has just left the study in which this page is being written. Her husband died two years ago. Her children are married. Her economic status, though modest, is secure. One statement of hers still echoes in the room as the door has closed. "I must find something to call forth my energies if I am to save my mental health." Human nature cannot be locked up for safe-keeping. It can be saved only by spending.

That truth, taught by the Great Physician, was retold a few years ago in the story of a modern doctor as portrayed in Lloyd Douglas' *Magnificent Obsession*. This fictional physician, mentally ill and physically run down, found a formula for curing himself through serving others so secretly that the transactions were freed from all self-consciousness and public recognition. Why did this novel go through edition after edition and its screen version break attendance records in more than one city? Such a record is not to be explained by any literary merit or exceptional dramatic interest. Its popular success was due to the fact that it struck something deeply responsive in the human heart.

Or turn from fiction to the case-history of a contemporary writer whose work has attained considerable distinction. Starting as a clergyman, he slipped into evil habits which dragged him down beyond the point of seeming possible recovery. How did he rehabilitate himself? By rest? By introspection? By sanatorium treatment? He tried all of these. But nothing availed until he began to put himself into other personalities through his rescue and relief activities. Recently at a certain college, where he is a visiting preacher, the wife of the president said that of all the men who came to that campus he seemed to have the most vital sense of God's reality.

Such contemporary situations illumine the scene in the Nazarene synagogue when Jesus, after announcing his program of giving health and help, anticipated his hearers' response by exclaiming, "Doubtless ye will say unto me this parable, Physician, heal thyself" (Luke 4. 23). That is precisely what men do say to anyone who comes offering a panacea or cure. We naturally assume that if a person has found a blessing or boon of any kind, he will first help himself with it. We are skeptical of any solution which does not appear to have worked in the case of him who offers it. Wise persons do not trust their estates to lawyers who cannot manage their own affairs, nor do they buy the "sure thing" suggested by the stock salesman who has just gone bankrupt. To such we say, "Physician, heal thyself."

Jesus recognized this natural reaction and seemed to endorse it. He himself ridiculed the Pharisee reformers who went about picking at the motes in the eyes of others without removing the beams in their own orbs. Healing and love and religion, like charity, should begin at home. So says the man on the street. So says the Man of Nazareth.

But the latter paradoxically declares that this healing of the self, though it starts at home, nevertheless must be headed outward in order to work inward. Elijah came as a prophet to aid Israel, but he went forth to assist a Sidonian woman. And Elisha, also a prophet in Israel, went out to cure Naaman, the Syrian (Luke 4. 25-27). That, Jesus implied, was the law of divine healing, applicable to individuals and to groups. Men heal themselves in the helping of others.

The rationality underlying this paradox begins to reveal itself in several directions. For one thing, in trying to help others we discover our own weaknesses and also our own curative powers. A homely parable, remembered from boyhood reading, is to the point here. An elephant, tethered to a ring in the floor of his cage, saw a

bit of hay fall just beyond the reach of his chain.
How was he to secure that food? Employing an
elephantine wisdom not always matched by the
"sons of light," he blew against the walls of his
cage, and the current of air returning brought the
hay to him.

Let that simple action be lifted to the human
realm and its implications are apparent. We send
out our energies in the service of others and there
comes back to us that which becomes the food for
our souls. We export our so-called civilization
to the backward regions of the earth, and we
thereby discover which of our modern develop-
ments have civilizing power. The Church of
Christ dispatches its missionary enterprise to the
non-Christian peoples and in the process finds out
which elements are empty ecclesiasticism and
which are spiritual dynamics. The experienced
foreign missionaries are better able to say what
are the saving fundamentals of our Christian faith
than are the "fundamentalists" at home. In fact,
an E. Stanley Jones, fresh from the spiritual
laboratory of India, is at this writing leading
a National Preaching Mission to revive American Christianity. Thus by spending ourselves for
others we find out which elements of our own
lives are worth keeping.

Moreover, we thereby get a fresh grip on our
own life possessions. "If ye have not been faith-

ful in that which is another's, who will give you
that which is your own?" (Luke 16. 12.) We
naturally think from the other end first, assuming
that fidelity and success in handling our own
affairs fit us for the trusteeship of others' interests. But Jesus reversed the direction of develop-
ment in asserting that stewardship of others
secures our possessions. Does Jesus' principle
work? Consider the home relationships. George
Herbert Palmer had such a reverent regard for
the rights and person of his wife, Alice Freeman,
that he said, "I never called her mine." He
looked upon himself as the guardian, not the possessor, of privileges. Thus did the love of Elizabeth Barrett and Robert Browning protect rather
than possess each other. As she put it:

> "the footsteps of thy soul
> Move still, O still beside me, as they stole
> Betwixt me and the dreadful outer brink
> Of obvious death, where I, who thought to sink
> Was caught up into love."

When husband or wife is such a trustee of the
other's interests, he or she wins permanent love,
whereas the mate whose possessive eye is always
watching to see whether he is getting the love
which belongs to him sooner or later begins to
feel cheated. Let a person enter a marital union,
a club membership, or a church fellowship with
an eye to the benefits to be received and it is not

long before he begins to feel that he is giving more than he is getting; on the other hand, he whose motive is that of trusteeship of the common interests feels a growing and satisfying sense of gratitude.

This securing of life's satisfactions by spending the self in stewardship of others is partly due to the "power that worketh in us" and also partly to the attraction which such an attitude exerts on others. As they were walking down street one day in Dublin, John Butler Yeats said to Padraic Colum, "Our liking for people is in inverse ratio to their sense of self-preservation."[1] The currents of love and co-operation flow in toward the person who empties himself of cautious concern for his own welfare. Men forget themselves into the affections of others. And love is the crowning feature of the life which is won by losing.

C. *Who Live by Dying*

Having seen that the paradox of winning life by losing is a working principle for this present world, we must also follow the force of it beyond the grave. When Peter asked what reward the disciples were to receive for having left all to follow him, Jesus assured them that they would be repaid "a hundredfold now in this time," and "in the world to come eternal life" (Mark 10. 30).

---

[1] William Lyon Phelps, *The Courage of Ignorance*, p. 27.

The Christian victory does not begin at death, but it requires eternity to complete it.

The Synoptic Gospels do not record Jesus as deliberately and explicitly discussing death, except when the question was brought to him. He assumed that his followers accepted the prevailing belief in a life beyond the grave. "If it were not so, I would have told you" (John 14. 2). When the Sadducees beset him with captious questions regarding the nature of immortality, he made it clear that he believed in the persistence of personality, freed from physical limitations (compare Mark 12. 18-27).

Jesus' life and thought ran on a track independent of the physical terminals of birth and death. He was concerned not with bodily birth, but with the "new birth," which was a spiritual beginning. And the death with which he mainly dealt was a spiritual, not a physical matter. He had a way of referring to certain persons as dead while they were still bustling busily about their affairs. When a prospective follower said, "Let me first go and bury my father," Jesus replied, "Let the dead bury their dead" (Luke 9. 60). Such language was figurative, to be sure, but it was also one of Jesus' ways of saying that a moving body is not evidence of what he called life. And in his parable of the Prodigal Son, the father is made to say upon the lad's return, "Let us eat, and make merry: for this my son was dead, and is alive again" (Luke 15. 24). The boy had been physically very much alive in that far country. In fact, we have heard prodigals who were taking their fling under similar conditions exclaim, "This is the life!"

In the light of Jesus' general attitude, it could be said that life and death come by degrees and not by physical suddenness. When a little human form is brought into the world, we say that a child is born. But only a small part of the life which is in any one of us now was begun on the day of our birth. Just a feeble current of energy pulsing through a few pounds of human flesh. enabling it to breathe and drink—such was life on that first day. The growth of a child is a series of new births.

Recall some of them. At six or thereabouts the little mind begins to be ushered into a world of letters and figures. In that tiny tot we see an adventurer on the threshold of a new life, a life which gives him fellowship with the noble figures of ancient time and of far-away lands, a life which adds so much to what he had before that it dwarfs that pre-book age into worthlessness. Consider the life of the poor yokel who can neither read nor write, who is shut into his own suspicions, feeding his starving mind on the scraps of information which fall from the tables of his

acquaintances. Of such a stupid, meager existence we would say at once, "That's not living."
Yet, of course, that illiterate fellow has all that
he had when he was born. No, the first birth, the
physical birth, does not make a man really to
live.

Or take another stage in the child's growth. At
nine the little girl is placed at the keyboard of a
piano. Those mysterious markings of a musical
score are explained to her. By those rather tire-
some exercises she begins to work her way into
a new world, a world of melodies and harmonies,
of delights and thrills which up to that time had
been completely unknown to her. Ask the
genuine musician how much this experience adds
to life. She will say, "Adds to life? Why, music
is my life!" And a real musician, looking upon
the musicless existence of a person shut away
from all its enjoyments, says, "That's not living."

Look again at another stage in life's expansion.
A young man of twenty-five meets a young
woman. Each has had interests and thrills. But
as they look into the eyes of each other they
realize that all which has gone before in their
careers is as nothing compared to what they mean
to each other. Each feels starved without the
other. Life ahead without the other looks to be
not worth living. The true lover does not cal-
culatingly feel that he is getting as good as he

gives. He feels that he is getting infinitely more than he gives, that he is adding immeasurably to his life. The ideal marriage is not merely a union to which children are born. It is a union in which husband and wife are reborn—reborn into a world of united interests, of shared joys, of vastly multiplied appreciations, of infinitely tender experiences. Husbands and wives who have lived long and happily together, who have climbed the steep ascent of success or walked through the valley of the shadow of adversity, who have come to rely more and more upon each other as the swift seasons roll—what do they say life was before they met and joined their hearts? Many of them would say with all sincerity and without a trace of sentimentality, "That single life wasn't living."

Realizing that growing life is a succession of new births, we are better prepared to understand what Jesus meant by a new birth. Just as around the illiterate man there lies unopened the world of books, as around the unmusical person there lies undeveloped the world of melody, as around the man who has not known a shared love there lies the world of home's happiness. so said Jesus, around the natural man there lies unexplored the rich world of spiritual things, of clearer insights, of widened sympathies, of deepened joys. Into that new life of the spirit we must be born. That is what he told Nicodemus on the housetop in Palestine.

And those who have accepted what he offers agree that Jesus did bring them life. They look back at their previous existence, try this and that daring simile to describe the change which Jesus has meant and then fall back on Paul's testimony, "When we were dead in sins, [God] hath quickened us together with Christ."

Professor William James, of Harvard, used to say that the average man uses only one tenth of his brain. And modern psychology speaks of unawakened people—persons in whom there are powers and instincts as yet not stirred to vital activity. The Master Mind of Galilee, looking upon the littleness of lives around him, realizing what the Creator expected of his human creatures, and what potentialities were in them, kept saying in substance to his fellow men, "Ye are not fully alive yet; ye must be born again."

Just as we are born by degrees, so we die by degrees. We say of a person in the grip of some progressive disease that "he is dying by inches." But this creeping paralysis or decay of the body does not constitute the only form of progressive death.

Yonder in the West is a young woman. In her student days music was her life. In it she lived and moved and had her being. She married a young lawyer, went West, and settled in a Nebraska village. At first her music was kept going by the momentum of her student passion for it. But no added stimuli came. No critically appreciative listeners were around her. Her husband's career in local politics began to absorb her. Her violin lay for long weeks untouched. She began to lose her touch, her technique, then her enthusiasm, then her taste. Ten years after her graduation she was very much alive in some regions of her mind. She knew politics. She was keenly alert to business futures, but musically she was almost dead.

Whitman once looking down with that compassionate heart of his at a poor woman of the streets whose giddy, frivolous life was over, realized that the cessation of breath in her body was only the completion of a dying process which had been going on for years. He exclaimed:

"Dead house of love—house of madness and sin,
    crumpled, crushed,
House of life, erstwhile talking and laughing—
    but, ah, poor house, dead even then,
Months, years, an echoing garnished house—
    but dead, dead, dead."

Or consider a certain young lawyer in this city. He came from a godly home. He was graduated from a college where the atmosphere is charged with idealism far above the average. He came to

New York with a most sensitive conscience and an eager spirit of helpfulness. He became intensely engrossed in his professional work. His week ends were spent in the country. The spiritual culture of his life was neglected. He was too busy to continue the setting-up exercises of his soul each morning. His moral sense is becoming flabby. When one looks at him now, he seems very much alive, a brisk, energetic, alert young member of the bar. But raise a religious question which once would have elicited a warm ringing enthusiastic assent, and hear his hard cynical comment, like a voice echoing through the marble corridor of a mausoleum. His polished urbane person is the abode of death which has laid its hand on a part of his nature once throbbing and vital. Thus we die by degrees.

In the light of Jesus' teaching the living and the dead are not two distinct groups divided by the single and sudden line of breath cessation. Living and dying are both processes of gradual transference. "Eternal life," as he used the expression, is a mode of existence so adjusted to unending things that it is independent of time and place. It is a state of being which his followers are to enter here on this earth in preparation for that day when physical death removes the bodily environment.

This matter of preparing for the hereafter may

be illustrated by way of an earthly parallel. Suppose that next autumn we were to move our residence to Nanking, China, for our future home. We have never been there. It is to us a strange country. We think it cannot possibly have the comforts and conveniences of New York or Denver. Therefore, in order to make the new life in China livable, we shall box up as many of our American possessions as possible and ship them with us. Thus we shall make our new home in Nanking as nearly as possible a duplicate of our house in New York. That is one way of preparing for our future living in China.

And that is precisely the way our primitive ancestors tried to prepare for the life after death. In the museum at Cairo may be seen the marvelous collections of exquisite equipment which Egyptian rulers like Tut-ankh-amen had placed in their tombs for their enjoyment of the future life. Likewise with the American Indian were buried his tomahawk and other treasures for his use in the Happy Hunting Ground.

But more intelligent modern folk recognize the futility of such naïve preparations. We know that we cannot take the things of the earth with us into the hereafter, that, as Paul said, "flesh and blood cannot inherit the kingdom of heaven." And is that not one of the primary reasons why we dread death? We so live and have our being in

the midst of material things that we become dependent upon them. Yet we know that we cannot take these things with us. Hence we can
hardly imagine how life will be worth living without them.

But there is another way by which we can prepare to move our home from America to China.
We can say: "Let's not try to take our American
things with us. Let us learn how to live in
Chinese fashion. Let us study the tastes and the
habits of that country so that we shall be 'at home'
when we settle in Nanking."

And this suggests the way Jesus tried to prepare his disciples for the life hereafter. His
formula was, "Lay up for yourselves treasures in
heaven." Learn to value heavenly things. Cultivate the taste for spiritual satisfactions. His followers are to look on the things which are unseen
and eternal until they come to enjoy them more
than the things which are seen and temporal.

This acclimation to the spiritually permanent
involves a dying to the physically temporal. "Except a grain of wheat fall into the earth and die,
it abideth by itself alone; but if it die, it beareth
much fruit. He that loveth his life loseth it; and
he that hateth his life in this world shall keep it
unto life eternal" (John 12. 24, 25). There must
be a letting go of the earthly in order to take hold
of the heavenly. There must be a dying of the

shell in order that the germ of the spirit may join
with the living forces of God. As a saintly old
lady put it to her pastor a few days before her
death, "Today I am in the land of the dying;
soon I shall be in the land of the living."

As the ground for confidence in this continuity
of personality, Jesus gave the integrity of God and
of himself. "Let not your heart be troubled: ye
believe in God, believe also in me" (John 14. 1).
In this interpretation of Jesus the fourth Gospel
gives a true reflection of his general attitude.
Having learned his reliability on this side of the
grave, his followers are to trust him for what lies
beyond.

But was Jesus a trustworthy interpreter of this
present life, or did his own death demonstrate the
fallacy of his faith? We shall not enter here on a
discussion of the resurrection records. Suffice it
to say that something happened nineteen centuries ago which made Jesus more of a living
force on the streets of Jerusalem after his crucifixion than on the day of the Triumphal Entry.
Something occurred which transformed the disciples of the slain Nazarene from defeated refugees
into radiant triumphant heralds of a risen Lord.
Was it all a delusion or illusion? Well, a false
report might last a few weeks, but the Church
which was founded on this report of the risen
Christ has continued and grown through the

centuries. If you can believe that a religious movement founded on a falsehood can produce generations of honest men, and flourish until it numbers almost 600,000,000 followers, then you are welcome to your opinion. But many of us find it harder to explain away the reports of Jesus' victory over death than to explain them. We therefore believe that death did not hold him.

A few years ago a distinguished scientist, probably America's most eminent geologist, was conducting a forum in an Eastern city. He had stated his belief that there is an Administration back of this universe which conserves its spiritual and personal values. In the question period which followed, an auditor asked, "How can you say that there is a trustworthy Divine Administrator who guarantees the permanence of spiritual values when a character like Jesus suffered defeat?" The answer was eloquent. Looking the inquirer in the eye, the speaker paused a moment and then said, "In the light of what Jesus accomplished during his days on the earth and in the centuries since, do you really think Jesus was defeated?"

No, he was the Winning Loser.

INDEX

Accumulation, unrighteous, 162
"Acts of God," 144
Addams, Jane, 187
American standard of living, 29
Anderson, Maxwell, 115
Annas, 69
Asceticism, 87, 165
Athleticism, 165
Augustine, Saint, 104

Backsliders, 90
Barrett, Elizabeth, 247
Barton, Bruce, 157
Beatitudes, 28, 33
Beethoven, 92
Bosworth, Dean Edward I., 25
Brotherhood, 162, 221
Browning, Robert, 46, 247
Bundy, W. E., 19
Burden-bearer, 57

Caiaphas, 69
Calvary, 185
Canaanitish woman, 31
Carrel, Alexis, 42, 85
Cavell, Edith, 235
Celibacy, 202
Centrifugal, 75
Centripetal, 75
Chesterton, G. K., 20, 37, 45, 84
Class distinctions, 160
Class legislation, 159
Colum, Padraic, 248
Campensation, present and future, 141
Confessional Synod, Proclamation of the, 26
Conqueror, confident, 116
Conscientious objectors, 231
Contemporary, eternal, 106

Corot, 58
Cosmic Christ, 78
Covetousness, 159
Crane, Dr. Frank, 117
Creators, constructive, 231
Cross against sword, 229

Death, spiritual, 249
Decay, spiritual, 198
Declaration of Independence, 83
Depravity, 188
Dickens, Charles, 122
Dictators, 29, 119
Discipline promotes liberty, 85
Dives, 61, 134, 160, 196
Dodgson, Charles, 46
Douglas, Lloyd, 243
Dreiser, Theodore, 232
Dynamics, spiritual, 246

Easton, Professor Burton Scott, 27
Ecclesiasticisms, 246
Eddington, A. S., 41, 42
Education, 101
Einstein, 28
Eliot, George, 67
Emerson's *Journal*, 241
Epicureanism, 240
Eternity, endless, 233
Ethiopia, 73, 121, 227
Experience precedes explanation, 40

Faith, 147
Father, living Heavenly, 179
Fatherhood, 141
Fatherliness, 182
"Father level," 27, 99
Fear, 182, 187, 194

261